EAT WHAT YOU LOVE, LOSE WHAT YOU HATE

LOSE WEIGHT WITHOUT GIVING UP YOUR FAVOURITE FOOD

DR S K LATH

Copyright © Dr S K Lath
All Rights Reserved.

This book has been self-published with all reasonable efforts taken to make the material error-free by the author. No part of this book shall be used, reproduced in any manner whatsoever without written permission from the author, except in the case of brief quotations embodied in critical articles and reviews.

The Author of this book is solely responsible and liable for its content including but not limited to the views, representations, descriptions, statements, information, opinions and references ["Content"]. The Content of this book shall not constitute or be construed or deemed to reflect the opinion or expression of the Publisher or Editor. Neither the Publisher nor Editor endorse or approve the Content of this book or guarantee the reliability, accuracy or completeness of the Content published herein and do not make any representations or warranties of any kind, express or implied, including but not limited to the implied warranties of merchantability, fitness for a particular purpose. The Publisher and Editor shall not be liable whatsoever for any errors, omissions, whether such errors or omissions result from negligence, accident, or any other cause or claims for loss or damages of any kind, including without limitation, indirect or consequential loss or damage arising out of use, inability to use, or about the reliability, accuracy or sufficiency of the information contained in this book.

Made with ♥ on the Notion Press Platform
www.notionpress.com

This book is dedicated to the pillars of my life, whose unwavering support and love have been the foundation upon which I stand.

To my parents, whose wisdom and guidance have shaped the person I am today. Your endless sacrifices and boundless love have been my greatest blessings.

To my beloved wife, Dr. Dolly Lath, who has been my constant companion and unwavering support. Your understanding and patience have given me the strength to pursue my dreams. Thank you for always being there, through every challenge and triumph.

To my wonderful children, Rajnandini, Mriganka, and Hrishiraj. Your joy and laughter have been the light of my life. I know I have taken time away from you to write this book, but I hope one day you will understand the passion and dedication behind it. You inspire me every day to be a better person and to strive for greatness.

To my patients, whose resilience and determination have motivated me to write this book. Your stories, struggles, and successes have been a source of inspiration and have driven me to create this guide. It is your trust and faith in me that have fueled my desire to help others achieve their health goals.

To Amritha, whose journey and contribution have been integral to this book. Your courage and commitment to change have not only transformed your life but have also provided invaluable insights that will help many others on their path to wellness. Your story is a testament to the power of determination and hope.

And finally, to the Almighty Shiv Baba, whose constant support and divine motivation have guided me throughout this journey. Your presence in my life has been a source of inner strength and peace. I am eternally grateful for your blessings and the clarity you have given me to accomplish this work.

Thank you to all of you for being my strength, my inspiration, and my guiding light. This book is a testament to your love, support, and the profound impact you have had on my life. I hope that this work will help others achieve their dreams and lead healthier, happier lives.

Contents

Contents

Contents

Preface

Obesity is often called the "mother of all diseases," and as a practicing physician, I have seen firsthand how it is intricately linked with numerous health problems, particularly diabetes. Over the years, I have encountered countless patients struggling with diabetes, and the common thread among the vast majority of them has been obesity. This realization has driven me to take a closer look at the root cause of diabetes and how addressing obesity can lead to significant health improvements and even the reversal of diabetes.

I wrote this book with a deep-seated conviction that by preventing or reversing obesity, we can make a substantial impact on diabetes management and prevention. My aim is to provide a comprehensive, practical, and scientifically-backed guide to weight loss that debunks common myths and misconceptions, making the journey towards a healthier life accessible to everyone.

One of the biggest hurdles my patients face is the plethora of myths surrounding obesity and weight loss. Many believe that losing weight requires extreme measures such as starvation or crash diets. This couldn't be further from the truth. Sustainable weight loss is about making informed, healthy choices consistently. Through this book, I aim to dispel these myths and provide a realistic and achievable path to weight loss.

Before embarking on any weight loss program, my patients often have numerous questions and concerns. They wonder if they will have to give up their favorite foods forever, if they will be able to maintain their new lifestyle, or if weight loss is even possible for them given their past struggles. This book addresses these questions, providing clear answers and actionable advice that can help anyone begin their weight loss journey with confidence.

Some of the key questions I aim to address in this book include:

1. **Do I have to starve myself to lose weight?**
2. **Are crash diets the only way to achieve quick results?**
3. **Can I still enjoy my favorite foods while losing weight?**
4. **What is the role of exercise in weight loss?**
5. **How do I stay motivated throughout my weight loss journey?**
6. **Is it possible to reverse obesity and related health conditions like diabetes?**
7. **How do I overcome plateaus and continue making progress?**
8. **What are the long-term strategies for maintaining a healthy weight?**
9. **How much time will it take to lose weight?**
10. **What is the guarantee of weight loss?**
11. **What is the cost per kilogram of weight loss?**

My ultimate goal with this book is to reverse obesity for approximately 1 lakh (100,000) people throughout my life. I believe that with the right knowledge, support, and dedication, anyone can achieve a healthy weight and improve their overall well-being. This book is not just a collection of dietary recommendations; it is a comprehensive guide that covers all aspects of weight loss, from nutrition and exercise to psychological and emotional well-being.

These six attributes are not only essential for losing weight but also for achieving any goal in life. In this book, I have described the journey of my patient, Amritha, who achieved her desired weight by embracing these attributes. She not only lost weight but also gained confidence and transformed her life in many ways.

Amritha's story is one of determination, hard work, and the right guidance. When she first came to me, she was struggling not just with her weight but also with her self-esteem and personal life. Through our sessions, she discovered that the key to her success lay in understanding the psychological aspects of her weight issues and addressing them with the right mindset and support.

The motive behind weight loss must be strong and personal. It's not enough to want to lose weight to look good; there has to be a deeper reason that drives you every day. Motivation is what keeps you going when the going gets tough. Belief in yourself and the process is crucial because without it, you will falter at the first sign of difficulty. Consistency in your efforts ensures steady progress. Mentorship provides the necessary guidance and course correction when needed. And finally, patience is essential because losing weight is a long-term journey and not a quick fix.

I dedicate this book to all my patients who have inspired me with their resilience and determination. Their journeys have been a source of learning and motivation for me, and it is my hope that this book will, in turn, inspire and guide many others towards a healthier, happier life.

Thank you for allowing me to be a part of your journey. I am confident that together, we can make a significant difference in the fight against obesity and diabetes.

How To Use This Book

Embarking on a weight loss journey is a significant step towards achieving a healthier and more fulfilling life. This book has been crafted to serve as your comprehensive guide, filled with valuable insights, practical advice, and real-life stories to inspire and motivate you. To maximize the benefits of this book and ensure a successful weight loss journey, here are some key steps on how to use it effectively:

1. **Read the Book 2-3 Times**: The first step is to read the book thoroughly, not just once but two to three times. Each read-through will deepen your understanding and reinforce the concepts, strategies, and insights provided. Repetition will help internalize the information, making it easier to implement in your daily life.

2. **Take Lessons from Each Chapter**: Every chapter in this book is designed to provide specific lessons and actionable steps. Pay close attention to the practical advice and tips offered. Take notes and highlight key points that resonate with you. Reflect on how you can apply these lessons to your personal weight loss journey.

3. **Focus on the Six Attributes**: One of the most crucial sections of this book is the explanation of the six attributes essential for weight loss: motivation, consistency, belief, knowledge, patience, and mentorship. These attributes are not only vital for weight loss but for achieving any significant goal in life. Understand and embrace these attributes fully, as they will guide you through the challenges and triumphs of your journey.

4. **Make Long-Term Goals**: Successful weight loss is not about quick fixes or short-term results. It's about

making sustainable changes that lead to long-term health and well-being. Set realistic and achievable long-term goals for yourself. Break these goals down into smaller, manageable steps, and celebrate your progress along the way.

5. **Preserve Consistency in Your Mind**: Consistency is key to achieving lasting results. Develop a routine that incorporates healthy eating habits, regular physical activity, and other positive lifestyle changes. Stay committed to your goals, even when faced with obstacles or setbacks. Remember that consistency over time leads to success.

6. **Know Everything About Diet and Nutrition**: Educate yourself about the fundamentals of diet and nutrition. This book provides detailed information about different food groups, macronutrients, micronutrients, and the role they play in your health. Understanding these concepts will empower you to make informed choices and create a balanced, nutritious diet.

7. **Read Materials in Italics and Follow Them**: Throughout the book, you will find materials written in italics. These are specific recommendations, tips, or instructions that are particularly important. Pay extra attention to these sections and follow the advice given. These italicized points are often practical steps you can take immediately to enhance your weight loss efforts.

8. **Avoid the Myths and Mistakes**: The journey to weight loss is often clouded by myths and misconceptions. This book addresses many common myths and mistakes people make. By recognizing and avoiding these pitfalls, you can stay on the right path and avoid unnecessary setbacks. Trust the information provided and steer clear of quick fixes or fad diets.

9. **Keep a Mentor for Guidance and Support**: Having a mentor or a support system can significantly enhance your weight loss journey. A mentor can provide guidance, encouragement, and accountability. Whether it's a healthcare professional, a friend, or a support group, find someone who can mentor you and help you stay motivated during tough times.

10. **Track Your Progress**: Regularly track your progress by keeping a journal or using a weight loss app. Document your meals, exercise routines, and any challenges or successes you experience. Tracking your progress helps you stay accountable and allows you to see how far you've come, which can be incredibly motivating.

11. **Stay Updated and Informed**: Weight loss and nutrition science are continually evolving. Stay informed about the latest research and trends in health and fitness. Reading reputable sources, attending workshops, or following trusted experts can provide you with new insights and keep you motivated.

12. **Stay Positive and Patient**: Weight loss is a journey that requires time and effort. Stay positive, even when progress seems slow. Celebrate small victories and learn from any setbacks. Patience is crucial, as lasting change doesn't happen overnight.

Remember, this book is not just a guide but a companion on your weight loss journey. Use it as a reference, a source of motivation, and a roadmap to achieving your health goals. Embrace the process, stay committed, and believe in your ability to transform your life. With dedication and the right approach, you can achieve and maintain a healthy weight, leading to a happier and more fulfilling life.

CHAPTER ONE

A Cry for Help

As the day wound down and the last rays of the sun bathed the hospital in a warm, golden glow, I glanced at the clock on my office wall. It was almost 6 PM, and I was eager to head home after a long day at the clinic. My mind was already drifting to thoughts of a quiet evening with my family when a soft knock on the door interrupted my reverie.

"Come in," I called, trying to mask my weariness with a polite tone.

The door opened slowly, and a woman stepped inside. She looked to be in her early thirties, with a forlorn expression that immediately tugged at my heartstrings. Her eyes, swollen from recent tears, met mine briefly before she looked away, as if ashamed of her own sorrow.

"Dr. Lath?" she asked hesitantly.

"Yes, that's me. How can I help you?" I responded, setting aside my thoughts of home and focusing on the patient before me.

She took a deep breath, her shoulders sagging as if the weight of the world rested upon them. "My name is Amritha," she began, her voice barely above a whisper. "I... I need your help."

I gestured to the chair across from my desk, and she sank into it with a heavy sigh. It was clear that whatever had brought her here was not just a physical ailment, but something that had deeply affected her spirit.

"What seems to be the problem, Amritha?" I asked gently, leaning forward to show her she had my full attention.

For a moment, she struggled to find her words. Then, as if a dam had burst, the story poured out of her in a torrent of pain and frustration. "My husband has filed for divorce," she said, her voice breaking. "He... he says he can't stand to be with me anymore because of my weight."

The raw pain in her eyes cut through me like a knife. I had seen many patients with various issues, but the emotional turmoil Amritha was experiencing was palpable. I took a deep breath, gathering my thoughts before responding.

"I'm so sorry to hear that, Amritha. That sounds incredibly difficult. Can you tell me more about what happened?"

She nodded, wiping away a tear that had escaped down her cheek. "We've been married for six years. When we got married, I was already a bit overweight, but it wasn't such a big issue. Over the years, I gained more weight, and it started to bother him. He tried to be supportive at first, but then he started making hurtful comments. Eventually, he just stopped caring and began avoiding me. Last week, he told me he's filing for divorce because he can't handle it anymore. He said I've let myself go and that I'm no longer the woman he married."

Her voice cracked, and she took a moment to compose herself. "I never thought he would leave me because of my weight. I thought our love was stronger than that."

My heart ached for her. Obesity is often a complex issue, intertwined with emotional and psychological factors. Amritha's story was a stark reminder of how deeply it can impact not just physical health but also relationships and self-esteem.

"Amritha, thank you for sharing that with me," I said softly. "I can't imagine how painful this must be for you. But I want you to know that you're not alone. We can work through this together."

She looked up at me, hope flickering in her eyes for the first time since she walked into my office. "Do you really think so? I've tried so many diets and exercise plans, but nothing seems to work."

I nodded, leaning back in my chair. "Weight loss is a challenging journey, and it's different for everyone. What's important is finding a plan that works for you, both physically and emotionally. We'll take this step by step, and I'll be here to support you throughout the process."

She took a deep breath, nodding slowly. "Okay, Dr. Lath. I trust you. I'm ready to do whatever it takes."

"Good," I replied, offering her an encouraging smile. "The first step is to understand your current health status and any underlying factors that might be contributing to your weight gain. We'll do a comprehensive assessment, and from there, we can develop a personalized plan."

As we talked, I could see the tension in her shoulders slowly easing. She was beginning to open up, to believe that change was possible. We scheduled a follow-up appointment for a full evaluation, and I assured her that together, we would find a path forward.

As Amritha left my office, I couldn't help but feel a deep sense of responsibility. Her story was one of many that highlighted the complex and often heartbreaking realities of obesity. But it also reminded me of why I chose this profession – to help people not just heal their bodies, but also mend their spirits.

That evening, as I finally headed home, I thought about the road ahead for Amritha. It would be a challenging journey, filled with ups and downs, but I was determined to help her find her way. And perhaps, through her story, I could also inspire others to believe in the possibility of transformation and the power of resilience.

The next day, I reviewed Amritha's medical history. She had struggled with her weight for most of her life. Her records showed numerous attempts at weight loss, from fad diets to intense workout regimens, all with little to no lasting success. It was clear that a different approach was needed – one that addressed not just the physical aspects of her condition, but also the emotional and psychological factors that were contributing to her weight gain.

When Amritha arrived for her follow-up appointment, I greeted her with a warm smile. "Good to see you again, Amritha. How are you feeling today?"

She smiled back, albeit weakly. "A bit better, I suppose. It helps to know that someone cares."

I nodded, understanding the importance of emotional support in her journey. "Let's start with a comprehensive assessment. This will help us understand your current health status and any underlying issues that might be contributing to your weight."

Over the next hour, we conducted a thorough evaluation. We discussed her eating habits, her level of physical activity, her stress levels, and her emotional well-being. Amritha was honest and open, revealing that she often turned to food for comfort, especially during times of stress and sadness. Her husband's criticism and eventual departure had only exacerbated these habits.

"Amritha, it's important to understand that weight gain is often linked to a variety of factors, including emotional ones," I explained gently. "We need to address these underlying issues as part of your weight loss journey."

She nodded, her eyes brimming with tears. "I just feel so overwhelmed. I don't know where to start."

"We'll take it one step at a time," I reassured her. "First, we'll focus on developing healthier eating habits. This doesn't mean depriving yourself of the foods you love, but rather finding a balanced approach that works for you."

We discussed various dietary options, emphasizing the importance of whole foods, portion control, and mindful eating. I encouraged her to keep a food diary to help identify patterns and triggers.

Next, we talked about physical activity. "Exercise doesn't have to be intense or time-consuming," I said. "It's about finding activities you enjoy and making them a regular part of your routine. Even a daily walk can make a big difference."

Amritha seemed more at ease as we talked, her initial despair slowly giving way to a sense of hope. "I used to enjoy swimming," she said thoughtfully. "Maybe I could start doing that again."

"That's a great idea," I replied. "Swimming is a fantastic low-impact exercise that's easy on the joints and great for overall fitness."

Finally, we addressed the emotional aspects of her journey. "It's important to have a support system," I said. "Whether it's friends, family, or a support group, having people to share your experiences with can make a big difference."

Amritha nodded, looking more determined. "I think I can do this, Dr. Lath. It's going to be hard, but I'm ready to make a change."

"I believe in you, Amritha," I said sincerely. "Remember, this is a journey, and it's okay to have setbacks. What's important is that you keep moving forward."

As she left my office, I felt a renewed sense of purpose. Amritha's story was just beginning, and I was committed to helping her succeed. Over the next few weeks, we worked closely together, adjusting her plan as needed and celebrating each small victory along the way.

There were times when Amritha struggled, when the old habits and doubts crept back in. But she persevered, fueled by a growing belief in herself and her ability to change. She began to see results, not just in terms of weight loss, but also in her overall well-being. Her energy levels improved, her mood lifted, and she started to rediscover the joy in life.

One day, about three months into her journey, Amritha walked into my office with a bright smile. "Dr. Lath, I have some news," she said excitedly. "I've lost fifteen pounds!"

"That's wonderful, Amritha!" I exclaimed, genuinely happy for her. "You've worked so hard, and it's paying off."

She nodded, tears of joy glistening in her eyes. "I couldn't have done it without

Throughout the night, I found myself unable to shake the weight of Amritha's story from my mind. As I lay in bed, thoughts of her struggles intertwined with reflections on the countless individuals facing similar challenges. The quiet of the night provided the perfect backdrop for introspection, and I couldn't help but dwell on the broader implications of obesity beyond just physical health.

Amritha's ordeal wasn't an isolated incident; it was a poignant example of the profound impact that obesity can have on every aspect of a person's life. Divorce, social stigma, loss of confidence, and loneliness were just a few of the many repercussions she faced – consequences that extended far beyond the number on the scale. And yet, her story was just one among millions, each one a testament to the far-reaching effects of weight-related issues.

As I pondered the enormity of the problem, a sense of urgency began to build within me. I couldn't ignore the fact that, as a doctor, I had a responsibility to address these issues not just on an individual level, but on a broader scale. The realization struck me like a bolt of lightning – I had a platform, a voice, and the knowledge to effect change. It was my duty to use these resources to help as many people as possible.

With each passing minute, the idea of writing a book on the subject grew more compelling. It wasn't just about sharing Amritha's story – it was about shining a light on the complex web of challenges faced by individuals struggling with obesity. It was about challenging societal norms and advocating for a more compassionate and inclusive approach to health and wellness. And it was about offering hope and practical solutions to those who felt trapped in a cycle of despair.

As the first light of dawn crept through the curtains, I made a silent vow to myself. I would embark on this journey not just for Amritha, but for every person who had ever felt the crushing weight of obesity bearing down on them. I would be their advocate, their champion, and their guide on the path to a healthier, happier life. And with that determination fueling my resolve, I set to work, penning the first words of what would become a manifesto for change – a beacon of hope in a world too often shrouded in darkness.

CHAPTER TWO

THE FIRST STEP

The next morning, as I arrived at the clinic, I was surprised to find Amritha already waiting outside my office. She was early, eager, and visibly anxious, but there was a brightness in her eyes that hadn't been there before. Her smile was genuine, and it was clear that she was ready to embark on this new journey.

"Good morning, Amritha," I greeted her warmly as I unlocked the door. "You're here bright and early."

"Yes, Dr. Lath," she replied, her excitement palpable. "I'm ready to start."

We settled into my office, and I could sense her nervous energy. She was full of expectations and hopes, and I wanted to ensure that her journey began on the right foot.

"Amritha," I began, "before we dive into the details, I want to talk about the reasons behind losing weight. It's important to understand that weight loss isn't just about looking a certain way or fitting into a smaller size. It's about improving your overall health and well-being."

She nodded, listening intently. "I understand. I know it's not just about my marriage."

"Exactly," I continued. "While stopping the divorce might be a powerful motivator, there are several other significant reasons to tackle obesity. Being overweight or obese can lead to a range of health issues. These include heart disease, type 2 diabetes, high blood pressure, and certain types of cancer. It can also lead to sleep apnea, osteoarthritis, fatty liver disease, and kidney disease."

Amritha's eyes widened as she absorbed the information. "I didn't realize it could affect so many areas of my health."

"It's true," I said. "And for women, obesity can also lead to conditions like polycystic ovary syndrome (PCOS), infertility, and complications during pregnancy. These are serious outcomes that can affect your quality of life and your future."

She looked down for a moment, processing the gravity of what I was saying. "I knew it was bad, but hearing all this makes it even more real."

"It is real," I affirmed. "But the good news is that by losing weight, you can significantly reduce these risks and improve your overall health. This is why it's crucial to have a clear, strong 'why' when you're trying to lose weight. It's not just about the immediate goal, like avoiding a divorce, but about creating a healthier, happier life for yourself in the long run."

Amritha nodded, her expression determined. "I see what you mean. I want to be healthy, not just for my marriage, but for myself."

"That's the right mindset," I encouraged her. "Having a clear and personal reason for losing weight helps maintain motivation, especially because losing weight is a long-term process. There will be challenges and setbacks, and having a strong 'why' will keep you focused and committed."

"Thank you for explaining that, Dr. Lath," she said. "I think it's important for me to keep reminding myself why

I'm doing this, especially on the tough days."

"Absolutely," I agreed. "Your 'why' will be your anchor. Now, let's talk about the first steps of your weight loss journey. We've already discussed healthy eating habits and incorporating physical activity into your routine. Today, we'll start implementing those changes."

Amritha leaned forward, eager to get started. "I'm ready."

"Great," I said, smiling at her enthusiasm. "Let's start with your diet. Remember, it's not about depriving yourself but making healthier choices. Focus on whole foods – fruits, vegetables, lean proteins, whole grains, and healthy fats. Try to avoid processed foods and sugary drinks."

She nodded, taking notes as I spoke. "I can do that. I'll also start keeping a food diary, like you suggested."

"That's an excellent idea," I replied. "It will help you track what you're eating and identify any patterns or triggers. For physical activity, start with something you enjoy. You mentioned you liked swimming – that's a great, low-impact exercise."

"I'll start going to the pool again," she said, a hint of excitement in her voice.

"Perfect. Aim for at least 30 minutes of activity most days of the week. It doesn't have to be all at once; you can break it up into shorter sessions if that's easier."

We spent the next hour going over her plan in detail, making sure she felt comfortable with each step. Amritha's determination was inspiring, and I could see that she was committed to making these changes.

"Remember, Amritha," I said as we wrapped up our session, "this is a marathon, not a sprint. There will be ups and downs, but each step you take is a step towards a healthier you. Keep your 'why' in mind, and don't hesitate to reach out if you need support."

She smiled, a mix of gratitude and resolve on her face. "Thank you, Dr. Lath. I feel hopeful for the first time in a long time."

As she left my office, I felt a deep sense of satisfaction. Amritha was taking control of her life, and I was honored to be part of her journey. Over the next few weeks, I watched her progress with a sense of pride and admiration. She faced challenges, of course – old habits were hard to break, and there were days when she felt discouraged. But she persevered, always coming back to her reasons for wanting to change.

Amritha's story is a powerful reminder that weight loss is about so much more than numbers on a scale. It's about reclaiming health, building confidence, and creating a future full of possibilities. Each patient's journey is unique, and finding their personal 'why' is crucial for maintaining motivation and achieving long-term success.

For anyone embarking on a weight loss journey, I offer this advice: Take the time to understand your reasons for wanting to lose weight. Write them down, reflect on them, and keep them close. They will be your guiding light on days when the path seems difficult, and they will remind you why every step forward is worth it.

Amritha's journey had just begun, and there was a long road ahead. But with a clear purpose and the right support, I was confident she would achieve her goals and transform her life. And through her story, I hoped to inspire others to find their own reasons to embark on the journey to better health.

SUMMARY:
Understanding the severe health risks associated with obesity, such as heart disease, diabetes, and PCOS, is crucial

in recognizing the importance of weight loss.

CHAPTER THREE

THE POWER OF WHY

The journey to weight loss, or any significant long-term goal, begins with a single, powerful step: understanding why you want to achieve it. For Amritha, and for anyone striving to overcome obesity or reach any other challenging milestone, a clear, compelling "why" is essential. This chapter delves into the importance of this foundational element, illustrating its power through Amritha's story and offering strategies to maintain motivation throughout the journey.

As the weeks passed, Amritha's determination remained steadfast. Her initial enthusiasm had evolved into a steady commitment, and the small victories she achieved along the way fueled her resolve. However, the road was not without its challenges. There were days when she felt exhausted, tempted to revert to old habits, or discouraged by slow progress. It was during these moments that her "why" became her anchor.

One afternoon, Amritha arrived at my office looking particularly weary. She had experienced a rough week, filled with stress at work and personal doubts. As she sat down, I could see the weight of her struggles etched on her face.

"Dr. Lath, I don't know if I can keep doing this," she confessed, her voice trembling with frustration. "Some days it feels like I'm fighting a losing battle."

I leaned forward, meeting her eyes with empathy and understanding. "Amritha, it's completely normal to feel this way. Every journey has its ups and downs, especially one as challenging as weight loss. But I want you to remember why you started this journey in the first place."

She nodded, her eyes brimming with tears. "I know, but sometimes it feels so hard to hold onto that."

"Let's revisit your 'why'," I suggested gently. "What is it that you truly want to achieve? What motivates you to keep going, even when it feels tough?"

Taking a deep breath, Amritha began to articulate her reasons. "I want to be healthy, to avoid all those diseases we talked about. I want to feel confident and happy in my own skin. And yes, I want to save my marriage, but more importantly, I want to prove to myself that I can do this. I want to be strong for my future."

"Those are powerful reasons, Amritha," I said, nodding. "Your 'why' is not just a single goal; it's a collection of deeply personal motivations that give you strength and direction. When you focus on these reasons, they can help you overcome the toughest obstacles."

Amritha's story is a testament to the importance of having a clear, compelling "why." This concept is not just crucial for weight loss but applies to any significant, long-term goal. Understanding and embracing your "why" provides the foundation upon which you can build and sustain your efforts.

The Importance of a Clear "Why"

1. **Motivation:** A strong "why" acts as a powerful motivator. When you know why you want to achieve a goal, it becomes easier to stay committed, even when the journey gets tough. For Amritha, knowing that her health, happiness, and self-worth were at stake gave her the drive to keep going.

2. **Direction:** Having a clear "why" gives you direction. It helps you make decisions that align with your goals and avoid distractions. When faced with a choice, you can ask yourself if it brings you closer to your "why."

3. **Resilience:** A compelling "why" builds resilience. It helps you bounce back from setbacks and continue moving forward. Amritha faced numerous challenges, but her "why" kept her resilient, allowing her to overcome obstacles and keep progressing.

4. **Focus:** A well-defined "why" keeps you focused on your goal. It helps you stay on track and avoid getting sidetracked by temporary temptations or setbacks. Amritha's focus on her health and well-being helped her stay committed to her weight loss plan.

Finding Your "Why"

For readers embarking on their own weight loss journey or any long-term goal, it's essential to identify and articulate your "why." Here are some steps to help you find and clarify your motivations:

1. **Reflect on Your Goals:** Take time to think about what you truly want to achieve. What are your long-term

aspirations? How do you want to feel? What changes do you want to see in your life?

2. **Dig Deep:** Ask yourself why these goals are important to you. Keep asking "why" until you reach the core of your motivations. For example, if your goal is to lose weight, ask why you want to lose weight. If the answer is to feel healthier, ask why feeling healthier is important to you, and so on.

3. **Write It Down:** Write down your "why" in clear, specific terms. This helps solidify your motivations and makes them more tangible. Amritha wrote her reasons in a journal, which she revisited whenever she felt discouraged.

4. **Make It Personal:** Your "why" should be deeply personal and meaningful to you. It should resonate with your values and aspirations. Avoid generic reasons; focus on what truly matters to you.

5. **Visualize Your Success:** Visualize what achieving your goal will look and feel like. Imagine the positive changes it will bring to your life. This mental image can reinforce your "why" and keep you motivated.

DR S K LATH

CHAPTER FOUR

Uncovering the Causes of Obesity

As Amritha's weight loss journey continued, we reached a crucial point in our sessions. It was time to delve deeper into understanding the root causes of her obesity. Identifying the underlying factors contributing to weight gain is essential for creating an effective and personalized treatment plan. This chapter explores the common causes of obesity and the importance of pinpointing these factors in every case.

During one of our sessions, I decided to shift the focus towards uncovering the possible causes of Amritha's obesity. While addressing her past weight loss attempts had been enlightening, understanding the root causes was equally important.

"Amritha," I began, "we've talked a lot about the methods you've tried for losing weight. Now, let's explore what might have contributed to your weight gain in the first place. Identifying these factors can help us create a more effective and sustainable plan."

Amritha nodded, looking thoughtful. "I never really thought about it that way, Dr. Lath. I've always just focused on losing the weight, not why I gained it."

"Exactly," I said. "Understanding the why behind your weight gain is crucial. Let's discuss some common causes of obesity and see if any resonate with your experience."

Common Causes of Obesity

1. **Genetics:**

Genetics play a significant role in obesity. Some people may have a genetic predisposition to gain weight more easily due to factors such as metabolism and fat storage. If there is a family history of obesity, it could indicate a genetic influence.

2. **Diet and Nutrition:**

Poor dietary habits are a leading cause of obesity. Consuming high-calorie, low-nutrient foods such as fast food, sugary drinks, and processed snacks can lead to excessive weight gain. Overeating and unhealthy eating patterns contribute significantly to obesity.

3. **Physical Inactivity:**

A sedentary lifestyle is a major contributor to obesity. With modern conveniences and technology, many people engage in less physical activity, leading to weight gain. Lack of exercise slows metabolism and reduces the body's ability to burn calories.

4. **Emotional and Psychological Factors:**

Emotional eating and psychological issues such as stress, depression, and anxiety can lead to overeating and weight gain. Food is often used as a coping mechanism, providing temporary comfort but leading to long-term health problems.

5. **Medical Conditions:**

Certain medical conditions, such as hypothyroidism, polycystic ovary syndrome (PCOS), and Cushing's syndrome, can contribute to weight gain. These conditions affect metabolism and hormone levels, making it difficult to maintain a healthy weight.

6. **Medications:**

Some medications, including antidepressants, antipsychotics, and corticosteroids, can cause weight gain as a side effect. It's important to discuss any medication-related weight changes with a healthcare provider.

7. **Socioeconomic Factors:**

Socioeconomic status can influence obesity rates. Limited access to healthy food options, safe places for physical activity, and healthcare resources can contribute to higher rates of obesity in lower-income communities.

8. **Environmental Factors:**

The environment in which a person lives can impact their weight. Factors such as the availability of unhealthy food options, lack of physical activity opportunities, and cultural attitudes towards food and body weight all play a role.

Amritha's Story: No Clear Cause

As we discussed these common causes, I could see Amritha reflecting on her own life and experiences. She seemed to be searching for connections, trying to understand what might have contributed to her weight gain.

"Dr. Lath," she finally said, "I've thought about everything we've discussed, but I can't pinpoint a specific cause. My family doesn't have a history of obesity, and while I've had my share of emotional eating, I don't think it's the main reason. I've been relatively healthy otherwise."

"That's perfectly okay, Amritha," I reassured her. "Sometimes, there isn't a single, clear cause of obesity. It can be a complex interplay of multiple factors, and for some people, the cause remains unclear. What's important is that we understand your unique situation and continue to focus on the steps we're taking to achieve your goals."

Summary: The Importance of Identifying the Cause of Obesity

Understanding the root causes of obesity is crucial for developing effective treatment plans. Common causes include genetics, poor diet, physical inactivity, emotional factors, medical conditions, medications, socioeconomic factors, and environmental influences. However, it's important to note that not everyone will have a clear or identifiable cause, as seen in Amritha's case. Despite this, recognizing and addressing potential contributing factors is key to achieving and maintaining a healthy weight.

By examining these causes, we can create personalized and sustainable strategies for weight loss. Whether the causes are clear or not, focusing on holistic and individualized approaches ensures the best chances for long-term success.

CHAPTER FIVE

COMMON MISTAKES ON THE WEIGHT LOSS JOURNEY AND HOW TO AVOID THEM

Embarking on a weight loss journey is a significant step towards better health and well-being. However, many people fall into common pitfalls that can hinder their progress and motivation. In this chapter, we will address these common mistakes and debunk the myths associated with them, providing a clearer path to sustainable weight loss.

1. How Much Will I Lose Within 3 Months?
Myth: "I will lose a large amount of weight quickly."

Reality: Weight loss is a gradual process and varies greatly among individuals.

Many people set unrealistic expectations for rapid weight loss. While it's possible to see significant changes within three months, it's essential to set realistic and healthy goals. According to the CDC, a safe and sustainable rate of weight loss is about 1-2 pounds per week. Over three months, this amounts to approximately 12-24 pounds.

Explanation: Rapid weight loss often leads to muscle loss, nutritional deficiencies, and other health issues. Focusing on gradual, steady weight loss is more sustainable and healthier in the long run.

2. Guarantee of Weight Loss

Myth: "I need a guarantee that I will lose weight."

Reality: There are no guarantees in weight loss, as it depends on numerous factors including diet, exercise, metabolism, and adherence to the plan.

No legitimate healthcare provider or weight loss program can guarantee specific results. Weight loss is influenced by individual differences and lifestyle factors. Programs that promise guaranteed weight loss are often misleading and can be dangerous.

Explanation: Effective weight loss requires a personalized approach, consistent effort, and patience. Setting realistic goals and maintaining a positive mindset are crucial for long-term success.

3. How Fast Will I Lose Weight?

Myth: "I will lose weight quickly if I follow this program."

Reality: The rate of weight loss varies and should be approached with patience.

Weight loss speed depends on starting weight, age, gender, metabolic rate, and adherence to the plan. Rapid weight loss is not sustainable and can lead to health complications.

Explanation: It's important to focus on building healthy habits rather than aiming for quick results. A balanced diet, regular exercise, and consistency will lead to sustainable weight loss.

4. Price Per Kilogram of Losing Weight

Myth: "I want to know the cost per kilogram of weight loss."

Reality: Weight loss is a holistic process and cannot be quantified purely in monetary terms.

Many people seek cost-effective solutions for weight loss. However, viewing weight loss in terms of cost per kilogram can lead to unhealthy practices and shortcuts.

Explanation: Investing in a healthy lifestyle, including nutritious food, fitness programs, and possibly professional guidance, is invaluable. The benefits of improved health, increased energy, and enhanced quality of life far outweigh the costs.

5. Relying Solely on Exercising and Overexercising

Myth: "Exercise alone will make me lose weight."

Reality: While exercise is crucial, diet plays an equally important role.

Exercise is essential for overall health, but relying solely on it for weight loss can be ineffective. Overexercising can lead to injuries, burnout, and does not compensate for poor dietary choices.

Explanation: A combination of regular physical activity and a balanced diet is the most effective approach to weight loss. According to the American Council on Exercise, 75-80% of weight loss is attributed to diet, with exercise contributing the remaining 20-25%.

6. Trying to Do It on a DIY Basis

Myth: "I can lose weight on my own without any help."

Reality: While self-motivation is key, guidance from professionals can enhance success.

Many people attempt to lose weight on their own but often lack the knowledge and support needed for sustainable results. Professional guidance provides personalized plans, accountability, and expertise.

Explanation: Consulting with healthcare providers, nutritionists, or fitness experts can provide the structure and support necessary for effective weight loss. A study published in the Journal of the American Medical Association found that participants who had professional support were more successful in losing weight and keeping it off.

7. Trying Every Diet and Exercise Available on the Internet

Myth: "I will try every popular diet and exercise I find online."

Reality: Switching between multiple diets and exercise programs can be counterproductive.

The internet is filled with fad diets and exercise routines that promise quick results. However, constantly changing plans can confuse your body and lead to inconsistent results.

Explanation: Finding a balanced, sustainable diet and exercise routine that works for you is crucial. Consistency is key to achieving long-term results. A study in Obesity Research found that long-term adherence to a single, well-structured plan is more effective than frequently changing diets and exercises.

8. Weighing Every Day and Getting Demotivated

Myth: "I need to weigh myself every day to track my progress."

Reality: Daily weigh-ins can lead to unnecessary stress and demotivation.

Weight fluctuates daily due to various factors such as water retention, food intake, and metabolic changes. Focusing too much on daily weight can lead to frustration and demotivation.

Explanation: It's better to weigh yourself weekly or bi-weekly to get a more accurate picture of your progress. Additionally, consider other metrics such as body measurements, how your clothes fit, and overall health improvements.

Additional Common Mistakes

Not Setting Realistic Goals: Unrealistic goals can lead to disappointment and quitting. Set achievable milestones and celebrate small victories along the way.

Ignoring Sleep and Stress Management: Sleep and stress significantly impact weight loss. Chronic stress and poor sleep can lead to hormonal imbalances and increased hunger, making it harder to lose weight.

Skipping Meals: Skipping meals can lead to overeating later in the day and disrupts metabolism. Regular, balanced meals help maintain energy levels and control hunger.

Relying on Supplements: Weight loss supplements are often marketed as quick fixes but can be ineffective or harmful. Focus on natural foods and a balanced diet.

Summary: Avoiding Common Pitfalls

In summary, embarking on a weight loss journey requires patience, realistic expectations, and a balanced approach. Avoiding common mistakes such as seeking quick fixes, relying solely on exercise, or frequently changing diets can improve your chances of success. Professional guidance, consistency, and a focus on sustainable lifestyle changes are crucial for achieving and maintaining weight loss.

Amritha's story is a testament to the power of understanding and avoiding these common pitfalls. By setting realistic goals, seeking professional support, and adopting a balanced diet and exercise routine, she was able to achieve her weight loss goals and improve her overall health.

Remember, weight loss is a journey, not a destination. Celebrate small victories, stay consistent, and focus on long-term health and well-being.

CHAPTER SIX

THE IMPORTANCE OF MOTIVATION

Everything was progressing smoothly with Amritha's weight loss journey. She was following the plan we had set out for her, steadily losing weight, and showing remarkable improvement. I was pleased with her dedication and the results she was achieving. My clinic was bustling with patients, ranging from those with diabetes to others dealing with various health issues, and I was kept quite busy.

Then, one day, my receptionist informed me that Amritha had missed several appointments and wasn't responding to our calls. This was unlike her, and I felt a pang of concern. I decided to intervene personally. I called Amritha and asked her to come in for a chat.

She arrived at my office looking somewhat downcast, a stark contrast to the motivated, upbeat woman I had been seeing. I welcomed her warmly, offering her a seat.

"Amritha, it's been a while. How have you been?" I asked, trying to keep the conversation light.

She sighed deeply. "Dr. Lath, I've been struggling. I don't know what's happened, but I feel like I've lost my way. The motivation I had before... it's just not there anymore."

I nodded, understanding that this was a critical moment in her journey. "Amritha, losing motivation is a common part of the process. It's something we all experience, especially when working towards long-term goals. Tell me, what's been going on?"

She hesitated, then began to open up. "At first, everything was going well. I was losing weight, feeling great, and following the exercise plan. But then, life got in the way. I had work pressures, family issues, and slowly, the routine we set started to feel like a burden. I started skipping workouts, eating unhealthy foods, and before I knew it, I just didn't want to do it anymore."

I listened intently, feeling her frustration and discouragement. "Amritha, I understand. It's not easy, and it's normal to feel overwhelmed at times. But remember why you started this journey. You had clear goals and a strong motive. Let's revisit that."

I explained to her the importance of breaking down the long journey into smaller, manageable milestones. "When we set out to achieve something significant, like losing weight or any other long-term goal, the motivation we initially have tends to wane over time. This is because, in the beginning, we're driven by the excitement of starting something new. But as weeks turn into months, that initial excitement fades. This is why it's crucial to break your journey into smaller parts. Celebrate each small victory, and let that fuel you to keep going."

Amritha nodded, her eyes reflecting a mixture of hope and doubt. "But how do I keep the motivation alive, Dr. Lath? It's so hard when progress seems slow."

I smiled, knowing this was a pivotal teaching moment. "There are several methods to stay motivated, Amritha. First, keep reminding yourself of your 'why' – the reason you embarked on this journey. Whether it's to improve your health, feel more confident, or avoid health complications, keep that reason at the forefront of your mind. Write it down, make it visible in your daily life."

Methods to Stay Motivated:

1. **Set Realistic Goals:**

"Instead of focusing on losing a large amount of weight, set small, realistic goals. Celebrate every kilo lost, every healthier food choice, and every workout completed. These small wins add up and keep you moving forward."

2. **Create a Support System:**

"Surround yourself with people who support and encourage you. Join a weight loss group, find a workout buddy, or stay in touch with others on a similar journey. Sharing your experiences and challenges can provide motivation and accountability."

3. **Track Your Progress:**

"Keep a journal of your weight loss journey. Note down what you eat, your workouts, and how you feel. Seeing your progress in writing can be incredibly motivating, especially on tough days."

4. **Reward Yourself:**

"Give yourself non-food rewards for achieving milestones. Treat yourself to a new outfit, a relaxing day out, or a movie night. These rewards can act as incentives to stay on track."

5. **Stay Positive:**

"Focus on the positive changes, no matter how small. Celebrate your improved energy levels, better mood, or looser clothes. Positive reinforcement is a powerful motivator."

6. **Adjust When Necessary:**

"Life happens, and sometimes you need to adjust your plans. If you miss a workout or indulge in a treat, don't be too hard on yourself. Get back on track as soon as you can. Consistency over time is what matters."

7. **Visualize Success:**

"Spend a few minutes each day visualizing your success. Imagine how you'll feel and look at your goal weight. This mental imagery can boost your motivation and keep you focused on your objectives."

8. **Seek Professional Help:**

"When things get tough, don't hesitate to seek help. Talking to a nutritionist, a personal trainer, or even a therapist can provide new insights and help you stay committed to your goals."

Rebuilding Amritha's Motivation

Amritha listened carefully, her expression gradually changing from one of despair to one of renewed determination. "I see, Dr. Lath. I think I can do this. I just need to break it down and not focus on the entire mountain but one step at a time."

"Exactly, Amritha. Remember, it's not about perfection, but progress. You've come so far already, and you have the strength to continue. Let's make a new plan together, focusing on small, achievable goals."

We spent the rest of our session setting new, realistic goals for Amritha and planning a strategy to help her stay motivated. By the end of our meeting, she looked more hopeful, ready to tackle her weight loss journey with renewed vigor.

As she left my office, I felt a sense of satisfaction. Helping patients like Amritha find their way again, reigniting their motivation, and watching them achieve their goals was why I loved my profession.

Summary: Staying Motivated

This chapter emphasizes the critical role of motivation in any long-term endeavor, especially weight loss. Losing motivation is normal, but by understanding your 'why,' setting realistic goals, creating a support system, and celebrating small victories, you can maintain the drive needed to achieve your goals. Remember, consistency and a positive mindset are key to long-term success. Just like Amritha, with the right approach and support, you too can stay motivated and reach your desired weight and beyond.

CHAPTER SEVEN

THE POWER OF A FOOD DIARY

Amritha had been on her weight loss journey for several months now, showing commendable progress and determination. However, during one of our routine check-ups, I noticed a change in her demeanor. She seemed worried and less enthusiastic than usual.

"Amritha, is everything alright?" I asked, concern evident in my voice.

She sighed heavily and looked down. "Dr. Lath, I don't know what's happening. I've been following the plan, but I'm not losing weight as expected. In fact, I haven't lost any weight in the last few weeks. I'm starting to feel really depressed about it."

I could see the frustration and disappointment in her eyes. "Amritha, let's talk through this. Sometimes, weight loss plateaus are a normal part of the journey. But first, let's go over your daily routine and dietary habits."

She hesitated before admitting, "I think I've been slipping up. I'm not always sticking to the dietary guidelines you gave me, and sometimes I eat more than I should, especially when I'm stressed or upset."

I nodded, understanding that maintaining a strict diet can be challenging, especially during tough times. "Thank you for being honest with me, Amritha. It's important to face these challenges head-on. I have a tool that might help you stay on track and be more mindful of your eating habits – a food diary."

I handed her a simple notebook. "In this diary, I want you to write down everything you eat and drink each day. Be as detailed and honest as possible. This isn't about judging yourself; it's about understanding your habits and identifying patterns that might be hindering your progress."

Amritha looked at the diary and then back at me. "But will this really help, Dr. Lath? I'm not sure I can stick to it."

I smiled reassuringly. "Yes, it can make a big difference. Keeping a food diary helps you become more aware of what and how much you're eating. It can highlight areas where you might be consuming extra calories without realizing it. Plus, it gives us a clear picture to work with and adjust your plan as needed."

We discussed the best ways to maintain the diary. "Write down everything right after you eat. Include portion sizes, how you're feeling when you eat, and any other details that seem relevant. Being honest is crucial – this diary is for your benefit. It's not about being perfect but being accurate."

Pre-requisites to Maintain a Food Diary:

1. **Honesty:**

"Be truthful about everything you consume. Remember, this diary is a tool for you, not something to impress others."

2. **Consistency:**

"Update your diary daily. The more consistent you are, the more useful the data will be."

3. **Detail:**

"Include portion sizes, times, and any emotional triggers that might have led you to eat."

4. **Review:**

"Look back at your entries regularly to spot patterns and areas for improvement."

I also explained that sometimes, despite doing everything right, weight loss can slow down or stop temporarily. "Think of it like a bamboo tree. For the first four to five years, you see no visible growth above the soil. But during this time, the bamboo is developing a strong root system underground. Then, seemingly out of nowhere, it starts growing rapidly, shooting up several feet in a short period. Our bodies can be similar. You might not see immediate results, but that doesn't mean progress isn't happening beneath the surface."

The Emotional Struggle and Breakthrough

A few weeks later, Amritha returned to my office, food diary in hand. She seemed a bit more hopeful, but still anxious about her progress.

"Dr. Lath, I've been keeping the diary as you suggested. It was tough at first, but it's become a bit easier. I've noticed some patterns, especially around my stress eating."

I looked through her diary and nodded approvingly. "This is excellent, Amritha. See, you've already identified one key area – stress eating. Now that we know this, we can work on strategies to manage it. For instance, finding alternative ways to cope with stress, like going for a walk, practicing meditation, or even talking to a friend."

We adjusted her plan based on the diary entries. Slowly but surely, Amritha began to see progress again. Her weight started to decrease, and more importantly, she felt more in control of her eating habits.

The Role of a Food Diary in Sustained Success

Maintaining a food diary isn't just about tracking what you eat; it's about understanding your relationship with food. It helps you become more mindful and intentional, rather than eating on autopilot. For Amritha, the diary became a source of empowerment. It allowed her to see her progress, adjust her habits, and stay accountable.

"Dr. Lath, I can't believe how much this diary has helped me. I feel more aware and in control now. It's not just about losing weight; it's about changing my lifestyle," Amritha said with a smile.

Her story is a testament to the power of mindfulness and the importance of staying motivated. There will always be ups and downs, but tools like a food diary can provide the guidance and structure needed to navigate the journey.

Summary: The Importance of a Food Diary

This chapter highlights the crucial role a food diary can play in achieving weight loss goals. By tracking everything you eat and drink, you gain valuable insights into your eating habits and can identify areas for improvement. Maintaining honesty, consistency, and detail in your diary is essential for it to be effective. Remember, weight loss is a long-term journey with inevitable plateaus. Like the bamboo tree, growth may not always be visible, but persistence will eventually yield results. Use the food diary as a tool to stay mindful, accountable, and motivated throughout your journey.

Amritha's journey, once again, underscores the importance of these tools and strategies in achieving lasting success. With determination, patience, and the right support, anyone can reach their goals and transform their life.

CHAPTER EIGHT

A Misstep in the Journey

One fine morning, as I sat in my OPD preparing for the day ahead, the door opened, and

Amritha walked in. I greeted her with a warm, "Good morning, Amritha." As I looked up from my desk, I noticed a striking change. She looked significantly slimmer, the weight loss was apparent and far beyond our expectations. But something was amiss. Her face was pallid, and her eyes lacked the sparkle I was accustomed to seeing. Her movements were slow, and she seemed to be in visible discomfort.

"Amritha, you've lost a lot of weight," I said, trying to sound positive. "But you don't look well. What's going on?"

Her eyes darted around the room, avoiding mine. She looked anxious and exhausted, a stark contrast to her usual self. I sensed that there was more to her condition than just physical symptoms.

"Please sit down," I urged, concerned. "Tell me what's been happening."

Amritha sat down slowly, her body almost collapsing into the chair. "Dr. Lath, I've been feeling really weak and in pain all over my body for the past few days. I thought it was just temporary, but it's getting worse. I'm also feeling very awkward... I haven't been able to look you in the eye because I feel guilty."

I listened carefully, trying to understand the underlying issue. "Guilty? Amritha, you can tell me anything. Let's figure this out together."

She took a deep breath, her voice trembling. "A few weeks ago, I met an old friend after a long time. She had lost about 7 kgs in just a month. I was amazed and asked her how she did it. She introduced me to a detox diet. She explained the full method – eating only salads, fruit juices, water, jeera water, lauki juice, and a few other things. She seemed so happy and energetic, so I thought I'd give it a try."

My heart sank as she continued. "Initially, I felt weak, but I was happy because I lost 5 kgs in 15 days. But then, the weakness became unbearable. I started feeling dizzy and couldn't concentrate on anything. I knew something was wrong, but I didn't want to admit it because I was thrilled with the weight loss."

Amritha's voice cracked as she continued, "I realize now that I made a mistake. I bypassed your advice and followed this extreme diet without thinking of the consequences. I feel so guilty and ashamed."

I reached across the desk and placed my hand gently on hers. "Amritha, it's okay. You're here now, and that's what matters. We all make mistakes. The important thing is to learn from them and move forward."

Her eyes welled up with tears. "Thank you, Dr. Lath. I just wanted to lose weight quickly. I didn't think about the harm it could do."

I nodded, understanding her desperation. "Rapid weight loss through extreme diets can be very harmful. It can lead to malnutrition, dizziness, weakness, and even long-term health issues. Our goal is not just to lose weight but to do so in a healthy and sustainable manner."

I took a moment to collect my thoughts and then explained the impact of such diets on her body. "When you deprive your body of essential nutrients, it goes into survival mode. You might lose weight initially, but it's mostly water and muscle, not fat. This weakens your body and can cause serious health problems."

Amritha listened intently, her guilt slowly turning into a resolve. "I understand now, Dr. Lath. I promise I won't do anything like this again. I will follow your advice diligently."

I smiled reassuringly. "That's the spirit. Let's focus on getting you healthy again. We'll start by treating your acute malnutrition and then gradually get you back on our standard dietary protocol."

I prescribed the necessary medications and supplements to help her recover from the malnutrition. We discussed a balanced diet plan that would nourish her body and support her weight loss journey without compromising her health.

As the days passed, Amritha's condition began to improve. The weakness and dizziness subsided, and she started to regain her strength. She followed the dietary plan meticulously and came for regular check-ups.

One afternoon, during a follow-up appointment, Amritha shared her thoughts with me. "Dr. Lath, I realize now that losing weight isn't just about looking good. It's about being healthy and feeling good from the inside out. I was so focused on the number on the scale that I forgot about my overall well-being."

I nodded, proud of her newfound understanding. "That's exactly right, Amritha. Weight loss is a journey, not a destination. It requires a holistic approach, considering both physical and mental health. Your motive for losing weight should be strong and personal. Motivation and belief in yourself and the process are crucial. Consistency in your efforts ensures steady progress, while supervision provides the necessary guidance. And finally, patience is essential because losing weight is a long-term journey."

Amritha smiled, a glimmer of hope returning to her eyes. "Thank you, Dr. Lath. Your support and guidance have made all the difference. I feel more confident and determined than ever."

Her words touched me deeply. It was moments like these that reminded me why I chose this profession. Helping my patients navigate their challenges and emerge stronger was incredibly rewarding.

Amritha's story was a powerful reminder that weight loss is not just about diet and exercise. It involves understanding the psychological aspects and having the right support system in place. Extreme diets and shortcuts might seem tempting, but they often lead to more harm than good. Sustainable weight loss requires a balanced approach, patience, and perseverance.

As Amritha continued her journey, she became an inspiration to others. Her determination and resilience were evident in every step she took. She shared her experiences with fellow patients, encouraging them to focus on their health and well-being rather than just the numbers on the scale.

Her transformation was not just physical; it was emotional and mental as well. She gained confidence, self-esteem, and a deeper understanding of her body. She learned to appreciate the journey and not just the destination.

One evening, during a casual conversation, Amritha said, "Dr. Lath, I can't thank you enough for everything you've done for me. You've been more than a doctor; you've been a mentor, a guide, and a friend."

I smiled warmly. "It's been my pleasure, Amritha. You've worked hard and stayed committed. I'm proud of you."

As I reflected on Amritha's journey, I realized that her story had the power to motivate and inspire others. It was a testament to the importance of having a clear motive, staying motivated, believing in oneself, being consistent, seeking supervision, and having patience. These attributes were not only essential for losing weight but for achieving any goal in life.

In the end, Amritha's journey was not just about losing weight; it was about finding herself, embracing her strengths, and becoming the best version of herself. Her story was a reminder that with the right mindset, support, and determination, anything is possible.

I hoped that sharing her story would resonate with others facing similar challenges and provide them with the motivation and guidance they needed. If Amritha could overcome her struggles and achieve her goals, so could they.

Amritha's journey was far from over, but she was now equipped with the knowledge, tools, and support to navigate it successfully. She had learned valuable lessons and grown stronger through her experiences. Her story was one of hope, resilience, and triumph, and I was honored to be a part of it.

CHAPTER NINE

Navigating the Maze of Diets – Finding the Right Path to Sustainable Weight Loss

In the quest for weight loss, patients often find themselves overwhelmed by the myriad of diet options available. From fad diets to scientifically-backed nutrition plans, the choices can be dizzying. Let's explore some of the most popular diets and understand why many individuals find themselves switching from one to another, often losing both motivation and the ultimate goal of weight loss in the process.

Popular Diets for Weight Loss

1. **Ketogenic Diet (Keto)**

- **Overview**: A high-fat, low-carbohydrate diet that aims to induce ketosis, a metabolic state where the body burns fat for fuel instead of carbohydrates.
- **Pros**: Rapid initial weight loss, reduced hunger, and potential improvements in blood sugar and cholesterol levels.
- **Cons**: Difficult to maintain, potential nutrient deficiencies, and possible side effects like the "keto flu."

2. **Paleo Diet**

- **Overview**: Focuses on consuming foods that were available to our Paleolithic ancestors, such as lean meats, fish, fruits, vegetables, nuts, and seeds.
- **Pros**: Encourages whole foods, eliminates processed foods, and can improve metabolic health.
- **Cons**: Restrictive, may lack certain nutrients, and can be expensive.

3. **Intermittent Fasting (IF)**

- **Overview**: Alternates between periods of eating and fasting. Common methods include the 16/8 method, where you fast for 16 hours and eat within an 8-hour window.
- **Pros**: Flexible, can lead to weight loss and improved metabolic health.
- **Cons**: Difficult for some to adhere to, can lead to overeating during eating periods, and may not be suitable for everyone.

4. **Mediterranean Diet**

- **Overview**: Emphasizes fruits, vegetables, whole grains, legumes, nuts, and healthy fats, particularly olive oil, along with moderate consumption of fish and poultry.
- **Pros**: Balanced, heart-healthy, and supported by extensive research.

- **Cons**: May require careful planning to ensure nutrient balance, and can be challenging for those used to high-fat, high-sugar diets.

5. **Low-Carb Diet**

- **Overview**: Limits carbohydrate intake while increasing protein and fat consumption.

- **Pros**: Effective for weight loss and blood sugar control.

- **Cons**: May cause initial side effects like headaches and fatigue, and can be challenging to maintain long-term.

6. **Vegan Diet**

- **Overview**: Excludes all animal products, focusing on plant-based foods such as fruits, vegetables, grains, nuts, and seeds.

- **Pros**: Can be very healthy, environmentally friendly, and ethical.

- **Cons**: Requires careful planning to avoid nutrient deficiencies, and can be restrictive.

The Cycle of Diet Switching

Many patients, eager for quick results, jump from one diet to another. Initially, they may see promising results, which fuels their motivation. However, as time passes, the restrictions and challenges of the diet become more apparent. This often leads to:

1. **Diet Fatigue**: The initial excitement wanes, and the diet feels more like a burden.

2. **Plateaus**: Weight loss slows down or stalls, which can be discouraging.

3. **Social Pressure**: Dietary restrictions can make social situations difficult, leading to feelings of isolation.

4. **Nutritional Deficiencies**: Extreme diets can lack essential nutrients, leading to health issues.

5. **Cravings**: Restrictive diets can lead to intense cravings, making it hard to stick to the plan.

These factors often lead to a cycle where individuals abandon their current diet and seek out a new one, hoping for better results. This constant switching can result in:

- **Loss of Motivation**: Frequent failures erode confidence and motivation.

- **Revenge Eating**: Feelings of deprivation can lead to binge eating or "revenge eating," where individuals consume large amounts of forbidden foods.

- **Weight Gain**: This cycle can cause weight gain, often exceeding the original weight, leading to feelings of frustration and hopelessness.

Even though many different types of diets are available for weight loss, the best diet is simple and healthy. It's easy to practice in the long term and helps maintain overall health. Given the pitfalls of constantly switching diets, it's crucial to adopt a sustainable, healthy diet. A balanced diet that provides adequate calories and nutrients not only supports weight loss but also maintains overall health. Here are the attributes of a normal, healthy diet:

1. **Nutrient Density**: A healthy diet includes a variety of foods that provide essential vitamins, minerals, and other nutrients. This ensures that the body gets what it needs to function properly.

2. **Metabolic Health**: Eating a balanced diet helps keep the basal metabolic rate (BMR) high, ensuring the body burns calories efficiently.

3. **Sustainable Weight Loss**: Gradual, consistent weight loss is more sustainable and healthier than rapid weight loss, which often leads to muscle and bone loss.

4. **Improved Energy Levels**: A well-rounded diet supports energy levels, making it easier to stay active and

engaged in physical activities.

5. **Mental Health**: Balanced nutrition supports brain health, improving mood and cognitive function, which is crucial for maintaining motivation and focus.

Guidelines for Achieving and Maintaining a Healthy Weight

Maintaining a healthy weight is crucial for overall well-being and can help prevent a range of chronic diseases. Here are some comprehensive guidelines to help you achieve and sustain a healthy weight:

1. **Eat Regular Meals**: Consistent meal times help regulate blood sugar levels and prevent overeating. Aim to eat every 3-4 hours to keep hunger at bay. Regular meals can also boost your metabolism and keep your energy levels stable throughout the day.

2. **Focus on Whole Foods**: Prioritize fruits, vegetables, whole grains, lean proteins, and healthy fats. Whole foods are rich in nutrients and fiber, which help you feel full and satisfied. Avoid processed foods high in sugar, unhealthy fats, and empty calories that can contribute to weight gain.

3. **Balanced Macros**: Ensure your diet includes a balanced mix of carbohydrates, proteins, and fats. Each macronutrient plays a vital role in maintaining health and supporting weight loss. Carbohydrates provide energy, proteins support muscle maintenance and growth, and fats are essential for hormone production and nutrient absorption.

4. **Hydration**: Drink plenty of water throughout the day. Staying hydrated supports metabolism and helps control appetite. Sometimes, thirst is mistaken for hunger,

leading to unnecessary snacking. Aim for at least 8-10 glasses of water daily, more if you are physically active.

5. **Mindful Eating**: Pay attention to hunger and fullness cues. Avoid eating when extremely hungry, as it can lead to overeating. Eat slowly and savor your food to enhance satisfaction and prevent overconsumption. Mindful eating encourages you to enjoy your meals and recognize when you are truly hungry or full.

6. **Portion Control**: Be mindful of portion sizes. Using smaller plates and bowls can help control portions and prevent overeating. Serving sizes in restaurants and packaged foods can be misleading, so learning to gauge appropriate portions is key to managing calorie intake.

7. **Regular Physical Activity**: Incorporate regular exercise into your routine. A combination of aerobic activities, strength training, and flexibility exercises supports overall health and aids in weight loss. Aim for at least 150 minutes of moderate aerobic activity or 75 minutes of vigorous activity each week, along with muscle-strengthening activities on two or more days a week.

8. **Good Sleep**: Ensure you get 7-9 hours of quality sleep each night. Poor sleep can disrupt hormones that regulate hunger and appetite, leading to weight gain. Establish a regular sleep routine and create a restful environment to improve sleep quality.

9. **Avoid Addictions**: Steer clear of addictive substances like alcohol, smoking, tea, and coffee. These can contribute to weight gain and other health issues. Reducing or eliminating these habits can improve your overall health and support your weight loss goals.

10. **Manage Stress**: Chronic stress can lead to emotional eating and weight gain. Practice stress-management techniques such as meditation, deep

breathing exercises, yoga, or engaging in hobbies. Finding healthy ways to cope with stress is essential for maintaining a healthy weight.

11. **Be Happy and Calm**: Maintaining a positive mindset and emotional well-being is crucial for overall health. Engage in activities that bring you joy and relaxation. Cultivating happiness and calmness can reduce stress and improve your relationship with food.

12. **Stay Consistent**: Consistency is key to achieving and maintaining a healthy weight. Small, sustainable changes over time are more effective than drastic, short-term measures. Create a routine that works for you and stick with it.

13. **Seek Support**: Having a support system can make a significant difference in your weight loss journey. Whether it's friends, family, or a weight loss group, having people to share your experiences and motivate you can boost your success.

14. **Educate Yourself**: Stay informed about nutrition and healthy living. Understanding the basics of healthy eating, reading food labels, and learning about the benefits of different types of foods can empower you to make better choices.

15. **Set Realistic Goals**: Set achievable and realistic weight loss goals. Aim for gradual weight loss, such as 0.5 to 1 kg per week. This approach is more sustainable and healthier than rapid weight loss.

16. **Monitor Progress**: Keep track of your food intake, physical activity, and weight. Journaling or using apps can help you stay accountable and identify areas for improvement.

By incorporating these guidelines into your daily routine, you can achieve and maintain a healthy weight.

Remember, the journey to a healthier you is a marathon, not a sprint. Celebrate your progress, no matter how small, and stay committed to your goals.

Conclusion

In conclusion, while the plethora of diet options can be tempting, it's essential to focus on a sustainable, healthy approach to weight loss. Extreme diets and frequent switching can lead to more harm than good, resulting in nutritional deficiencies, loss of motivation, and even weight gain.

A balanced diet that provides adequate calories and nutrients is key to maintaining a high BMR, supporting overall health, and achieving long-term weight loss. By embracing a holistic approach that includes regular meals, whole foods, balanced macros, hydration, mindful eating, portion control, and physical activity, individuals can achieve their weight loss goals and improve their overall well-being.

Remember, the journey to weight loss is not just about shedding pounds; it's about building a healthier, happier life. With the right mindset, support, and sustainable habits, you can achieve your goals and maintain them for the long term.

CHAPTER TEN

Understanding Body Types and Personalized Weight Loss Strategies

As Amritha's journey continued, I began to notice something essential about her: she had a unique body type that influenced her weight loss process. Understanding one's body type can significantly impact the approach to diet and exercise, making the journey more effective and sustainable. In this chapter, we delve into the concept of body types, using Amritha's story to illustrate how personalized strategies can lead to better results.

The Three Primary Body Types

The human body is generally classified into three primary types: ectomorph, mesomorph, and endomorph. However, many people are a combination of these types. Understanding these body types helps in tailoring diet and exercise plans to suit individual needs.

1. **Ectomorph**: Ectomorphs are typically lean and long with difficulty building muscle mass. They have a fast metabolism, which makes gaining weight a challenge.

Characteristics:

- Lean build with small joints and long limbs
- Fast metabolism
- Difficulty gaining weight (both muscle and fat)
- Narrow shoulders and hips

Diet and Exercise Recommendations:

- **Diet**: Ectomorphs should focus on a calorie-dense diet rich in carbohydrates and proteins. Healthy fats should also be included to ensure sufficient calorie intake. Frequent meals and snacks are beneficial.

- **Exercise**: Strength training with heavy weights and low repetitions is ideal for building muscle. Compound movements like squats, deadlifts, and bench presses are effective. Cardio should be limited to avoid burning too many calories.

2. **Mesomorph**: Mesomorphs have a natural athletic build and can gain muscle easily. They have a more balanced body composition and a moderate metabolism.

Characteristics:

- Muscular and well-defined body
- Naturally strong with broad shoulders
- Gains muscle easily but also prone to gaining fat if not careful
- Medium metabolism

Diet and Exercise Recommendations:

- **Diet**: A balanced diet with a good mix of proteins, carbohydrates, and fats works well for mesomorphs. They should ensure they get enough calories to support muscle growth while avoiding excess fat gain.

- **Exercise**: A combination of strength training and cardio is effective. Mesomorphs can benefit from both compound and isolation exercises. Cardio should be moderate to maintain cardiovascular health and manage fat levels.

3. **Endomorph**: Endomorphs tend to have a higher body fat percentage and gain weight easily. They have a slower metabolism and often struggle with weight loss.

Characteristics:

- Higher body fat with a rounder physique
- Gains weight easily, especially fat
- Wider waist and hips
- Slower metabolism

Diet and Exercise Recommendations:

- **Diet**: Endomorphs should focus on a diet that is high in protein and low in carbohydrates and fats. Emphasizing vegetables, lean meats, and whole grains can help manage weight. Portion control and meal timing are crucial.

- **Exercise**: Regular cardio exercises, such as running, cycling, or swimming, are essential to burn calories. Strength training with lighter weights and higher repetitions can help build muscle and boost metabolism.

Amritha's Body Type: Meso-Endomorph

Amritha's body type is a combination of mesomorph and endomorph characteristics, known as meso-endomorph. She has the potential to gain muscle relatively easily but also tends to gain fat if her diet and exercise are not carefully managed.

Characteristics of Meso-Endomorph:

- Can build muscle easily like a mesomorph
- Prone to gaining fat like an endomorph
- Needs to be careful with diet to avoid excess fat gain

- Benefits from a balanced approach to diet and exercise
Amritha's Personalized Plan:

To ensure that Amritha achieves her weight loss goals while maintaining her muscle mass, I developed a tailored plan that incorporates the best of both worlds from mesomorph and endomorph strategies.

Amritha's Journey: A Personalized Approach

Amritha's story highlights the emotional and physical struggles many face in their weight loss journey. Her transformation required not just a change in her diet and exercise but also a shift in her mindset and understanding of her body.

Diet Plan for Amritha:

1. **Balanced Nutrient Intake**: Amritha's diet included a balanced intake of proteins, carbohydrates, and fats. Lean proteins such as chicken, fish, tofu, and legumes were emphasized to support muscle maintenance and growth.

2. **Carbohydrate Management**: To manage her weight effectively, Amritha focused on complex carbohydrates such as whole grains, vegetables, and fruits, which provided sustained energy without causing spikes in blood sugar.

3. **Healthy Fats**: Healthy fats from sources like avocados, nuts, seeds, and olive oil were included to ensure she received adequate calories and nutrients for overall health.

4. **Meal Timing and Portion Control**: Amritha ate smaller, frequent meals throughout the day to keep her metabolism active and prevent overeating

CHAPTER ELEVEN

BUILDING TRUST AND DISCOVERING HIDDEN OBSTACLES

As Amritha's weight loss journey continued, I noticed a growing sense of trust and openness in our sessions. We had built a solid foundation of understanding and mutual respect. This bond was about to take a significant step forward, marked by a special invitation that would reveal an important aspect of her eating habits.

One afternoon, as our session was wrapping up, Amritha looked at me with a warm smile and a hint of excitement in her eyes. "Dr. Lath, I have a request," she began hesitantly. "My birthday is coming up this weekend, and I would love for you and your family to join me for lunch at my home."

I was touched by her invitation. It was a clear sign that she trusted me not just as her doctor, but as a friend and ally in her journey. "I'd be honored, Amritha," I replied. "My family and I would love to celebrate your birthday with you."

The day of the lunch arrived, and my family and I made our way to Amritha's home. It was a modest but cozy place, filled with the warmth of her personality. Amritha greeted us at the door, her face glowing with happiness and anticipation.

"Welcome, Dr. Lath! Welcome, everyone!" she exclaimed, ushering us inside. The table was set with an array of delicious-looking dishes, and the aroma of home-cooked food filled the air.

As we settled down to eat, Amritha's mother joined us, serving generous portions of each dish. The conversation flowed easily, filled with laughter and stories. However, as the meal progressed, I noticed something important about Amritha's eating habits.

Amritha had been chatting animatedly, clearly enjoying the company and the food. But I observed that she had waited until she was extremely hungry before starting to eat. When she finally did begin, she ate quickly and consumed a large portion.

After we finished our meal and moved to the living room for dessert, I decided it was time to address what I had noticed. "Amritha," I began gently, "thank you for inviting us today. The food was wonderful, and it was a pleasure to celebrate with you. But I noticed something during lunch that I think we should discuss."

Amritha looked slightly puzzled but nodded. "Of course, Dr. Lath. What is it?"

"I noticed that you waited until you were very hungry before starting to eat, and then you ate quite quickly," I explained. "This is something that many people do without realizing it, but it can actually hinder your weight loss efforts."

She looked thoughtful. "I guess I never really thought about it that way. I just eat when I feel hungry."

"That's common," I said. "But here's the problem: when you wait until you're extremely hungry, your brain doesn't send the satiety signals quickly enough. By the time your brain registers that you've had enough to eat, you've already consumed more than your body needs."

Amritha nodded slowly, absorbing this information. "That makes sense. I do often feel very full after meals."

The Science Behind Eating Habits

To help Amritha and our readers understand better, I explained the science behind this phenomenon. When you eat in a hurry because you're very hungry, your brain's satiety signals—the signals that tell you you've had enough—are delayed. This delay can lead to overeating, as you continue to consume food until your brain finally catches up and tells you to stop.

To avoid this, it's important to eat at regular intervals and not wait until you're famished. Eating small, frequent meals every three to four hours can help maintain a steady level of hunger and prevent overeating. By eating when you feel a little hungry, rather than very hungry, you can better control portion sizes and avoid consuming excess calories.

Guidelines for Healthy Eating Habits

1. **Eat Regularly:**

Plan to eat every three to four hours to keep hunger at bay and maintain steady energy levels. This prevents the extreme hunger that leads to overeating.

2. **Listen to Your Body:**

Pay attention to your body's hunger cues. Eat when you start to feel hungry, and stop eating when you're comfortably satisfied, not stuffed.

3. **Mindful Eating:**

Practice mindful eating by savoring each bite and eating slowly. This allows your brain to catch up with your stomach and send satiety signals in time.

4. **Avoid Skipping Meals:**

Skipping meals, especially breakfast, can lead to extreme hunger and poor food choices later in the day. Make sure to start your day with a nutritious breakfast to set the tone for healthy eating throughout the day.

5. **Balanced Meals:**

Ensure your meals are balanced, including a variety of nutrients from different food groups. Include lean proteins, whole grains, healthy fats, and plenty of fruits and vegetables.

6. **Portion Control:**

Be mindful of portion sizes. Use smaller plates and bowls to help control portions and avoid overeating.

7. **Hydration:**

Drink plenty of water throughout the day. Sometimes, thirst is mistaken for hunger, leading to unnecessary snacking.

8. **Avoid Distractions:**

Avoid eating while watching TV, working, or engaging in other distractions. Focus on your meal to enjoy the experience and recognize when you're full.

A Deeper Understanding of Eating Patterns

As we continued our discussion, I realized that this was an excellent opportunity to delve deeper into the broader implications of eating patterns and the importance of maintaining a healthy routine. Many people, like Amritha, adopt certain eating habits without understanding their impact on weight and overall health.

"Amritha," I said, "this brings us to another important point. Our bodies have a natural biological clock, also known as the circadian rhythm, which regulates our sleep-wake cycle and many other physiological processes, including digestion and metabolism."

"That sounds interesting," Amritha said. "Can you tell me more about it?"

"Of course," I replied. "Our bodies are designed to be active during the day and rest at night. This means that our digestive system and metabolism are more efficient during the daytime. However, modern lifestyles often disrupt this natural rhythm. Many people skip breakfast, eat a large lunch, and then have a heavy dinner late at night, sometimes even indulging in midnight snacks."

Amritha nodded, clearly recognizing these habits. "I used to do that a lot," she admitted. "Especially skipping breakfast and then eating a big dinner."

"You're not alone," I reassured her. "But this pattern can lead to metabolic imbalances and weight gain, as well as other gastrointestinal issues like acidity, bloating, and indigestion. To support your body's natural rhythms, it's important to have a nutritious breakfast, a moderate lunch, and a light dinner. Try to avoid late-night eating and stimulants like tea or smoking."

Additional Advice for Healthy Eating Habits

1. **Don't Skip Breakfast:**

Breakfast is the most important meal of the day. It provides the energy your body needs after the overnight fast and sets the stage for healthy eating throughout the day.

2. **Avoid Heavy Dinners:**

Aim to have your largest meals earlier in the day when your metabolism is more active. Keep dinner light and avoid eating late at night.

3. **Limit Snacking:**

Be mindful of snacking, especially late at night. If you need a snack, opt for healthy options like fruits, nuts, or yogurt.

4. **Social Eating:**

When eating with friends or at parties, be aware of portion sizes and try to eat mindfully. It's easy to overeat in social settings, so take smaller portions and savor your food.

5. **Avoid Shared Plates:**

Sharing plates can make it difficult to gauge how much you've eaten. Use your own plate to better control portion sizes and avoid overeating.

6. **Gifting and Temptations:**

Avoid storing large quantities of sweets, chocolates, and other high-calorie treats at home. If you receive them as gifts, consider sharing them with others or distributing them to avoid temptation.

7. **Mindful Eating:**

Avoid eating while watching movies or engaging in other activities. Focus on your meal and chew slowly to recognize when you're full and avoid overeating.

8. **Smaller, Frequent Meals:**

Eating small, frequent meals can help regulate hunger and prevent overeating. This approach can also help reduce stomach size over time, making it easier to control portions.

Personal Experience at Amritha's Lunch

Reflecting on the lunch at Amritha's home, I realized that many of the habits we discussed were common among my patients. It's easy to fall into patterns that seem harmless but can significantly impact weight and health. By sharing Amritha's story and the guidelines we discussed, I hoped to help others recognize and address these habits.

"Thank you for pointing that out, Dr. Lath," Amritha said sincerely. "I'll definitely work on eating more regularly and being mindful of my hunger cues."

"I'm glad to hear that, Amritha," I replied. "Remember, the key is to make small, sustainable changes. Over time, these changes will add up and make a big difference in your health and weight loss journey."

Summary: Identifying and Addressing Eating Habits

This chapter highlights the importance of identifying and addressing hidden eating habits that can hinder weight loss efforts. By understanding the science behind hunger and satiety, and following guidelines for regular, mindful eating, individuals can better control portion sizes and prevent overeating. Additionally, maintaining a balanced diet and respecting the body's natural rhythms can support overall health and weight management. Recognizing and adjusting these habits is a crucial step in any successful weight loss journey.

CHAPTER TWELVE

THE ILLUSION OF "FAT-FREE" AND "SUGAR-FREE" FOODS

One warm summer evening, my wife and I decided to visit a shopping mall. As we strolled through the bustling corridors, a familiar voice called out from behind.

"Dr. Lath!"

I turned around to see Amritha, her face beaming with excitement. We exchanged greetings, and she insisted on treating us to the nearby ice cream parlor. Amritha, who had made remarkable progress in her weight loss journey, was keen to share a special treat with us.

"Dr. Lath, you must try this," she said enthusiastically, pointing to a sign that read "Fat-Free and Sugar-Free Ice Cream." Knowing I was diabetic, she eagerly suggested, "It's healthy and perfect for both of us!"

I smiled and thanked her for her kind gesture but politely declined, not wanting to dampen her spirits. We sat down, and she enjoyed her treat, her joy contagious. However, I knew I had to address the misconceptions surrounding such "healthy" options during our next consultation.

The Truth About "Fat-Free" and "Sugar-Free" Foods

At her next visit, Amritha arrived with her usual smile, but I could see a hint of curiosity in her eyes. I welcomed her and decided it was time to discuss an important topic.

"Amritha, do you remember the ice cream we had the other night?" I began.

"Yes, it was delicious, wasn't it?" she replied cheerfully.

I nodded. "It was, but I want to explain something about these 'fat-free' and 'sugar-free' labels."

Amritha listened attentively as I continued. "These labels can be misleading. Many food companies market products as 'fat-free' or 'sugar-free,' giving the impression that they are healthier options. However, the reality is often quite different."

The Deceptive Labels

I explained that "fat-free" foods are often laden with sugar and other additives to compensate for the loss of flavor that fat provides. Similarly, "sugar-free" products may contain artificial sweeteners and other chemicals that can have various health implications.

"For example," I said, "many fat-free items contain trans fats, which are even more harmful than the regular fats they replace. Trans fats can increase bad cholesterol (LDL) and lower good cholesterol (HDL), significantly raising the risk of heart disease."

Amritha looked concerned. "I had no idea. I thought I was making healthier choices."

The Nutritional Reality

To drive the point home, I asked her to compare the nutritional labels of a regular ice cream and the fat-free version she had enjoyed. We found that the fat-free version had nearly the same calorie count, and in some cases, even higher due to added sugars and fillers.

"See this," I pointed out, "the fat-free ice cream has more sugar to make up for the lack of fat. And the artificial sweeteners and additives in sugar-free products can cause digestive issues and other health problems."

Amritha nodded, clearly absorbing the information. "So, what should I do, Dr. Lath?"

A Better Approach to Diet

"It's important to choose whole, minimally processed foods," I advised. "Instead of focusing on 'fat-free' or 'sugar-free' labels, aim for a balanced diet with natural ingredients. Moderation is key."

I shared examples from various studies and articles that highlighted the misconceptions of such products. For instance, a study published in the "Journal of the American College of Nutrition" revealed that people consuming fat-free snacks often ended up eating more calories overall because they believed they were eating healthier options.

Additionally, a review in "Current Diabetes Reports" found that artificial sweeteners, while calorie-free, could alter gut bacteria and lead to weight gain and metabolic issues.

Amritha's Understanding

Amritha's face reflected a mixture of surprise and understanding. "Thank you for explaining this, Dr. Lath. I see now that I need to be more cautious about these so-called healthy options."

I smiled, feeling a sense of accomplishment. "Remember, it's not just about losing weight, but about maintaining overall health. Making informed choices will help you stay healthy in the long run."

Real-World Examples

To illustrate further, I shared some real-world examples with Amritha:

Hidden Dangers in Sugar and Fat Substitutes: What to Avoid

In the quest for healthier eating and weight loss, many people turn to alternatives to sugar and fat, hoping to cut calories without sacrificing taste. Unfortunately, not all substitutes are created equal. Some ingredients marketed as "sugar-free" or "low-fat" can actually contain high calories or unhealthy components that undermine your health goals. Here, we'll explore some common substitutes that should be approached with caution.

1. **Artificial Sweeteners**

Artificial sweeteners like aspartame, sucralose, and saccharin are popular sugar substitutes found in many "sugar-free" products. These sweeteners are many times sweeter than sugar, so they are used in small amounts, theoretically reducing calorie intake. However, there are several concerns associated with their use:

- **Metabolic Effects**: Studies suggest that artificial sweeteners may interfere with the body's ability to regulate blood sugar, potentially increasing the risk of metabolic syndrome and type 2 diabetes.

- **Cravings**: Some research indicates that artificial sweeteners may actually increase cravings for sweet and high-calorie foods, leading to overeating.

- **Digestive Issues**: These sweeteners can cause gastrointestinal problems, including bloating, gas, and diarrhea in some individuals.

2. **High-Fructose Corn Syrup (HFCS)**

HFCS is a common sweetener in many processed foods and beverages. It is derived from corn starch and consists of both glucose and fructose. While it is often marketed as a natural product, HFCS has been linked to several health issues:

- **Weight Gain**: HFCS is associated with increased fat accumulation, particularly in the liver, which can lead to obesity and related diseases.

- **Insulin Resistance**: Consuming large amounts of HFCS can cause insulin resistance, a precursor to diabetes.

- **Appetite Regulation**: HFCS does not stimulate insulin secretion or enhance the production of leptin, the hormone responsible for signaling fullness, potentially leading to overeating.

3. **Agave Nectar**

Agave nectar is often marketed as a healthy, natural alternative to sugar. It has a low glycemic index, meaning it doesn't cause rapid spikes in blood sugar levels. However, agave nectar has some significant downsides:

- **High Fructose Content**: Agave nectar is composed of 70-90% fructose, much higher than the fructose content in HFCS. High fructose intake is linked to increased fat storage, insulin resistance, and fatty liver disease.

- **Caloric Content**: Despite being touted as a healthier option, agave nectar is still high in calories and can contribute to weight gain if not consumed in moderation.

4. **Coconut Sugar**

Coconut sugar is derived from the sap of the coconut palm and is often promoted as a healthier sugar alternative. It contains small amounts of nutrients like iron, zinc, calcium, and potassium. However, it's important to consider the following:

- **Caloric Density**: Coconut sugar has a similar calorie content to regular sugar, which means it can contribute to calorie excess if not used sparingly.
- **High Sucrose Content**: Coconut sugar is about 70-80% sucrose, which is essentially the same as table sugar and has similar effects on blood sugar and insulin levels.

5. **Brown Rice Syrup**

Brown rice syrup is a sweetener derived from brown rice. It is often found in health foods and marketed as a healthier alternative to high-fructose corn syrup. However, it has its own drawbacks:

- **High Glycemic Index**: Brown rice syrup has a high glycemic index, meaning it can cause rapid spikes in blood sugar levels.
- **Arsenic Contamination**: Brown rice syrup can be contaminated with arsenic, a toxic element that can pose serious health risks over time.

6. **Date Sugar**

Date sugar is made from ground, dried dates and is often marketed as a natural sweetener. While it does contain some fiber and nutrients, there are some considerations to keep in mind:

- **Caloric Content**: Date sugar is high in calories and can contribute to weight gain if consumed in large amounts.
- **Glycemic Impact**: Although it contains fiber, date sugar can still impact blood sugar levels, especially when used in large quantities.

7. **Fat-Free Products**

Many products labeled as "fat-free" or "low-fat" are often perceived as healthier options. However, these products can be misleading:

- **Added Sugars**: To improve taste, fat-free products often have added sugars, which can increase calorie content and negate any fat reduction benefits.

- **Lack of Satiety**: Fat is essential for feeling full and satisfied. Removing fat from products can lead to overconsumption of these foods, as they may be less satisfying.

8. **Chips and Snacks**

Many "baked" or "fat-free" chips often contain more sodium and other preservatives to enhance flavor, which can lead to high blood pressure and other health issues.

9. **Desserts**

Sugar-free desserts often contain sugar alcohols like sorbitol or maltitol, which can cause bloating, gas, and diarrhea.

10. **Dairy Products**

Fat-free yogurts frequently have added sugars to improve taste, which can contribute to insulin resistance and weight gain.

11. **Soft Drinks**

Diet sodas are sugar-free but contain artificial sweeteners like aspartame, which have been linked to headaches, dizziness, and even a higher risk of metabolic syndrome.

Practical Tips for Avoiding Unhealthy Substitutes

1. **Read Labels Carefully**: Always check ingredient lists for hidden sugars, artificial sweeteners, and unhealthy fats. Ingredients like HFCS, aspartame, and partially hydrogenated oils are red flags.

2. **Choose Whole Foods**: Opt for whole, unprocessed foods whenever possible. Natural foods like fruits, vegetables, nuts, seeds, and lean proteins are the best choices for a healthy diet.

3. **Moderation is Key**: Even natural sweeteners and healthier fats should be consumed in moderation. Overindulging in any sweetener can lead to excess calorie intake and weight gain.

4. **Educate Yourself**: Understanding the impact of different ingredients on your health can help you make better choices. Stay informed about the potential risks associated with various sugar and fat substitutes.

5. **Use Natural Sweeteners Sparingly**: If you choose to use natural sweeteners like honey or maple syrup, do so sparingly. These sweeteners still contain sugars and should be treated as such.

6. **Healthy Fats**: Incorporate healthy fats like avocados, nuts, seeds, and olive oil into your diet. These fats are essential for overall health and can help you feel full and satisfied.

7. **Monitor Portions**: Pay attention to portion sizes, especially when consuming high-calorie foods. Using smaller plates and measuring out portions can help control calorie intake.

8. **Stay Hydrated**: Sometimes thirst is mistaken for hunger. Drinking water throughout the day can help manage hunger and prevent overeating.

By being mindful of these common pitfalls and making informed choices, you can better navigate the world of sugar and fat substitutes and maintain a healthier, more balanced diet.

The Emotional Connection

Reflecting on our conversation, Amritha looked relieved. "I've learned so much today. It's not just about avoiding certain foods, but understanding what I'm putting into my body."

I nodded. "Exactly. The goal is to nourish your body, not just to lose weight. Every choice you make should be towards better health."

As she left my office, I felt a sense of fulfillment. Helping Amritha and others like her make informed decisions about their diet was a crucial part of their journey. It wasn't just about the numbers on the scale, but about fostering a healthier, more informed relationship with food.

Summary

This experience with Amritha highlighted the importance of being aware of food marketing tactics. "Fat-free" and "sugar-free" labels can be deceiving, often leading to the consumption of unhealthy additives and hidden calories. By focusing on whole, natural foods and understanding nutritional labels, one can make better dietary choices that support long-term health and well-being.

Through Amritha's story, we learn the value of informed decision-making in our dietary habits. It's a lesson that resonates not just with her, but with anyone striving to lead a healthier life.

CHAPTER THIRTEEN

Respecting Our Stomach - The Gateway to Health

We often overlook the incredible role our stomach plays in our overall well-being. Our stomach, along with our tongue, gives us the most delightful sensations and pleasures of life through the experience of taste. Yet, astonishingly, we neglect it, treating it with far less care than it deserves. Instead of nurturing this vital organ, we often use it as a dumping ground, filling it with all kinds of junk and disregarding the quality and timing of our food intake.

Most of us are guilty of skipping breakfast, fasting through the day, and then indulging in heavy dinners and midnight snacks. This routine is entirely opposite to what nature intended for our bodies. The natural rhythm of day and night is designed to optimize our bodily functions, including digestion. During the day, when we are active and our metabolism is at its peak, we should be consuming the majority of our food. In contrast, nighttime is for rest and repair, a time when our digestive system should also be winding down.

However, our modern lifestyle often disregards these natural rhythms. We often either skip or take a light breakfast. In some Marwadi communities like ours, we typically have "chai and roti" for breakfast, which should be avoided. Tea can prevent the absorption of key nutrients, suppress appetite, and inhibit gut enzymes. This practice leads to insufficient nutrition in the morning, setting a poor foundation for the rest of the day and often resulting in compensating with large, heavy meals late in the evening. A nutritious breakfast is essential for maintaining balanced energy levels and overall health.. This pattern not only leads to weight gain but also to a host of gastric issues.

Frequent midnight snacks, desserts, and heavy meals disrupt our digestive system, leading to symptoms like bloating, acid reflux, and indigestion. In turn, we rely on medications to relieve these symptoms, further burdening our body.

The Importance of Loving Our Stomach

Our stomach is more than just an organ; it's the core of our physical well-being, the place where the journey of nourishment begins. It tirelessly processes the food we consume, extracting nutrients and providing energy to keep us going. Yet, we often neglect its needs, filling it with junk food, irregular meals, and not giving it the love and care it deserves.

Imagine your stomach as a loyal friend who works around the clock, without breaks, to keep you alive and healthy. This friend asks for so little in return – a balanced diet, regular meals, and a bit of consideration. How often do we forget to show gratitude to this unsung hero of our body?

When we skip meals, overeat, or consume unhealthy foods, we're not just harming our stomach, but we're also betraying a friend who relies on us to treat it right. It's like planting a beautiful garden and then neglecting to water it, expecting it to flourish on its own.

Loving our stomach means being mindful of what we eat and how we eat. It's about savoring our food, choosing nutritious options, and maintaining a consistent eating schedule. It's about understanding that every bite we take is a message to our stomach – a message of care or neglect.

Amritha, learned to love her stomach through her weight loss journey. She used to eat mindlessly, often consuming whatever was quick and easy, regardless of its nutritional value. This habit led to weight gain and various health issues. It wasn't until she started paying attention to her stomach's needs that she began to see real change.

Amritha began to treat her stomach with the respect it deserved. She stopped skipping meals and started her day with a nutritious breakfast. She chose whole foods over processed snacks, understanding that what she ate directly affected her health and well-being. She realized that loving her stomach was about more than just losing weight; it was about nurturing her body and giving it the best chance to thrive.

In time, Amritha's relationship with food transformed. She no longer saw meals as a chore but as an opportunity to nourish her body and show gratitude to her stomach. This shift in mindset not only helped her achieve her weight loss goals but also brought a sense of peace and contentment to her life.

Loving our stomach is a journey of self-respect and care. It's about recognizing the vital role our stomach plays in our overall health and treating it with the kindness it deserves. By choosing to eat mindfully and nutritiously, we honor this incredible organ and pave the way for a healthier, happier life.

So, let's make a promise to our stomach today. Let's pledge to feed it with love, nourish it with care, and appreciate the incredible work it does for us every day. Because when we love our stomach, we're not just taking care of an organ; we're taking a profound step toward loving ourselves.

Guidelines for Healthy Eating Habits

1. **Start with a Nutritious Breakfast**: Breakfast is the most important meal of the day. A nutritious breakfast kickstarts your metabolism, provides energy for the day, and prevents overeating later. Include a balance of protein, fiber, and healthy fats.

2. **Eat Regular, Balanced Meals**: Aim to eat small, balanced meals every 3-4 hours. This keeps your metabolism active, prevents extreme hunger, and stabilizes blood sugar levels.

3. **Focus on Quality**: Choose whole, unprocessed foods. Include plenty of fruits, vegetables, lean proteins, whole grains, and healthy fats. Avoid foods high in sugar, unhealthy fats, and artificial additives.

4. **Avoid Heavy Dinners**: Consume lighter meals in the evening. Your metabolism slows down at night, making

it harder to digest heavy foods. Opt for a light dinner and avoid eating at least 2-3 hours before bedtime.

5. **Stay Hydrated**: Drink plenty of water throughout the day. Water aids in digestion and helps maintain the body's natural balance. Avoid sugary drinks and excessive caffeine.

6. **Mindful Eating**: Pay attention to what and how you eat. Chew your food thoroughly and eat without distractions. This helps in better digestion and prevents overeating.

7. **Avoid Midnight Snacks**: Late-night eating disrupts your digestive system and can lead to weight gain. If you feel hungry, opt for a light, healthy snack like a piece of fruit or a handful of nuts.

Conclusion:

Our modern lifestyle often leads us to make poor dietary choices that overburden our stomach. By making conscious changes to our eating habits, focusing on the quality and timing of our meals, and treating our stomach with the care it deserves, we can significantly improve our health and well-being.

Respecting our stomach is a crucial step towards achieving and maintaining a healthy weight and overall health. Let's commit to loving our stomach, feeding it nutritious foods at the right times, and breaking the cycle of neglect. Your stomach is not a dumping ground; it's the gateway to a healthier, happier life. Embrace this change, and your body will thank you.

In the story of Amritha, she learned this valuable lesson through her journey. She realized that treating her stomach with respect and care was key to her successful weight loss and improved health. Let her journey inspire you to make positive changes in your own life. Take care of your stomach, and it will take care of you.

CHAPTER FOURTEEN

DISCOVERING THE ESSENTIALS OF NUTRIENT ABSORPTION

The Unexpected Lesson

Amritha's weight loss journey had brought us closer, both as doctor and patient, and as friends. Our frequent sessions were not just about tracking her progress, but also about delving into the underlying issues that had contributed to her obesity. One session, in particular, became a turning point in our understanding of nutrition and health.

It was a rainy afternoon when Amritha walked into my office, her usual bright smile somewhat dimmed. She took a seat and sighed deeply.

"Dr. Lath, I've been following the diet and exercise plan strictly, but I still feel exhausted all the time," she said, frustration evident in her voice. "I eat healthy foods, but it's like my body isn't getting what it needs."

I nodded, understanding her concern. "Amritha, sometimes it's not just about what we eat, but how we eat it. Our bodies need to absorb the nutrients from our food to function optimally. Let's explore your eating habits in more detail."

As we discussed her daily routine, I noticed several patterns that could be affecting her nutrient absorption. I decided to dig deeper by sharing a personal story that highlighted the importance of how we consume our food.

A Story of Transformation

Years ago, I had a patient named Priya, a bright young woman in her late twenties. She had come to me with severe fatigue, frequent illnesses, and an inability to lose weight despite a seemingly perfect diet. Her case had baffled her previous doctors, but I sensed there was more to the story.

During one of our sessions, Priya broke down in tears. "I just don't understand, Dr. Lath. I eat all the right foods, but I still feel so weak and tired. It's affecting my work and my life."

We began to meticulously examine her eating habits, meal timings, and lifestyle. It turned out that Priya often ate her meals in a rush, skipped breakfast regularly, and drank large amounts of coffee throughout the day to keep her energy levels up. She also preferred processed foods for convenience.

"Priya," I gently explained, "our bodies are incredibly complex. It's not just about eating healthy foods, but also about how we consume them and how our body processes them. There are common mistakes that can prevent us from fully utilizing the nutrients in our food."

Through a step-by-step process, we worked on changing Priya's eating habits. She started eating slowly, paying attention to her hunger and fullness cues, and including a variety of foods in her diet. Gradually, her energy levels improved, and she began to feel better both physically and emotionally.

Inspired by Priya's transformation, I knew I needed to share these insights with Amritha and others who might be struggling with similar issues.

Common Mistakes That Hinder Nutrient Absorption:

1. **Eating Too Quickly:** Consuming food too rapidly can hinder digestion and absorption as the body doesn't have enough time to break down food properly.

2. **Poor Food Combinations:**

Food combinations can significantly impact the way nutrients are absorbed and utilized by our bodies. While some combinations enhance nutrient absorption, others can hinder it, leading to nutritional deficiencies or other health issues. Here are some irrational food combinations that should be avoided:

1. **Iron and Calcium-Rich Foods**: As mentioned, iron absorption can be hampered by consuming it with calcium-rich foods. For example, eating a spinach salad (rich in iron) with a dairy-based dressing (rich in calcium) can reduce iron absorption.

2. **High-Fiber Foods with Minerals**: Consuming high-fiber foods, such as whole grains, with mineral-rich foods can interfere with the absorption of essential minerals like zinc, magnesium, and calcium. The phytic acid in fiber can bind to these minerals, making them less available for absorption.

3. **Acidic Foods with Starchy Foods**: Eating acidic foods (like tomatoes or citrus fruits) with starchy foods (like potatoes or bread) can impair the digestion of starch. The acidic environment can interfere with the enzymes needed to break down starch, leading to digestive discomfort.

4. **Protein and Carbohydrate-Rich Foods**: Combining protein (like meat) with carbohydrate-rich foods (like potatoes) can slow down digestion. Proteins and carbohydrates require different enzymes and pH levels for digestion, and consuming them together can cause digestive issues such as bloating and gas.

5. **Fruit with Meals**: Fruits digest quickly and can ferment if eaten with slower-digesting foods, leading to gas and bloating. It's generally better to eat fruits on their own or before meals rather than after.

Common Medications and Foods to Avoid

Certain foods can interfere with medications, reducing their effectiveness or causing adverse reactions. Here are some common examples:

1. **Grapefruit and Medication**: Grapefruit can interfere with the metabolism of various medications, including statins (used for lowering cholesterol), some blood pressure medications, and certain anti-anxiety drugs. It can increase the concentration of the medication in the bloodstream, leading to potential toxicity.

2. **Leafy Greens and Blood Thinners**: Foods high in vitamin K, such as spinach, kale, and other leafy greens, can interfere with blood thinners like warfarin. Vitamin K can promote blood clotting, counteracting the effect of the medication.

3. **Dairy Products and Antibiotics**: Calcium in dairy products can bind with certain antibiotics (like tetracycline

and ciprofloxacin), reducing their absorption and effectiveness. It's recommended to take these antibiotics at least two hours before or after consuming dairy.

4. **Alcohol and Medication**: Alcohol can interact with many medications, including antidepressants, painkillers, and antihistamines, enhancing their sedative effects and leading to increased drowsiness or dizziness. It can also reduce the effectiveness of medications like antibiotics and blood pressure medications.

5. **Tyramine-Rich Foods and MAOIs**: Monoamine oxidase inhibitors (MAOIs), used to treat depression, can have dangerous interactions with foods high in tyramine, such as aged cheeses, cured meats, and fermented foods. This combination can lead to a hypertensive crisis.

Practical Tips for Avoiding Irrational Food Combinations

1. **Separate Iron and Calcium-Rich Meals**: To maximize iron absorption, consume iron-rich foods separately from calcium-rich foods. For example, have a spinach salad with a lemon-based dressing (vitamin C enhances iron absorption) and save dairy products for a different meal.

2. **Pair High-Fiber Foods Wisely**: When consuming high-fiber foods, be mindful of mineral intake. Consider taking mineral supplements or consuming mineral-rich foods at different times.

3. **Stagger Protein and Carbohydrates**: To ease digestion, try to consume proteins and carbohydrates in separate meals. For instance, have a protein-rich breakfast and a carbohydrate-rich lunch.

4. **Eat Fruits Alone**: Enjoy fruits as a snack between meals rather than immediately after meals to prevent digestive issues.

5. **Check Medication Labels**: Always read medication labels and consult with your healthcare provider or pharmacist about potential food interactions. Follow their guidelines to avoid adverse effects.

By understanding and avoiding irrational food combinations, you can optimize nutrient absorption and improve overall health. Additionally, being aware of food and medication interactions is crucial for ensuring the effectiveness of treatments and avoiding unwanted side effects.

3. **Overcooking Vegetables:** Overcooking can destroy vital nutrients in vegetables, reducing their nutritional value.

4. **Skipping Meals:** Irregular eating patterns can disrupt the body's ability to absorb nutrients efficiently.

5. **Relying on Processed Foods:** Processed foods often lack essential nutrients and are high in additives and preservatives that can interfere with nutrient absorption.

6. **Inadequate Chewing:** Not chewing food thoroughly can result in larger food particles that are harder for the stomach to digest, leading to poor nutrient absorption.

7. **Insufficient Fiber Intake:** Low fiber intake can negatively impact gut health, which is crucial for nutrient absorption.

Best Methods to Maximize Nutrient Absorption:

1. **Eat a Balanced Diet:**

- Ensure your diet includes a variety of foods from all food groups: proteins, carbohydrates, fats, vitamins, and minerals. A diverse diet ensures you get a wide range of nutrients.

2. **Chew Food Thoroughly:**

- Chewing food properly breaks it down into smaller particles, making it easier for digestive enzymes to work effectively and improve nutrient absorption.

3. **Incorporate Healthy Fats:**

- Some vitamins, such as A, D, E, and K, are fat-soluble and require dietary fat for proper absorption. Include healthy fats like avocados, nuts, seeds, and olive oil in your meals.

4. **Combine Foods Wisely:**

- Pair vitamin C-rich foods (like citrus fruits, tomatoes, and bell peppers) with iron-rich plant foods (like spinach and beans) to enhance iron absorption.

5. **Cook Vegetables Lightly:**

- Lightly steaming or sautéing vegetables can help preserve their nutrient content. Some nutrients, like lycopene in tomatoes, are better absorbed when cooked.

6. **Include Probiotics and Prebiotics:**

- Probiotics (found in yogurt, kefir, sauerkraut) and prebiotics (found in garlic, onions, bananas) support a healthy gut microbiome, which is crucial for nutrient absorption.

7. **Stay Hydrated:**

- Water is essential for digestion and nutrient transport. Drink plenty of water throughout the day, but avoid excessive water intake during meals to not dilute digestive juices.

8. **Avoid Antinutrients:**

- Certain compounds in foods, like phytates in grains and legumes, can inhibit nutrient absorption. Soaking, fermenting, or sprouting these foods can reduce their antinutrient content.

9. **Regular Meal Timing:**

- Maintain regular meal times to keep your digestive system functioning optimally. Irregular eating can disrupt digestive processes and hinder nutrient absorption.

10. **Moderate Use of Caffeine and Alcohol:**

- Excessive caffeine and alcohol can interfere with the absorption of certain nutrients like calcium, iron, and vitamins. Moderate your intake to avoid these issues.

11. **Opt for Whole Foods:**

- Choose whole, unprocessed foods over refined and processed options. Whole foods retain more of their natural nutrients and fibers, which aid in nutrient absorption.

12. **Mindful Eating:**

- Pay attention to what and how you eat. Eating in a relaxed state and being mindful of your food can improve digestion and nutrient absorption.

13. **Supplement Wisely:**

- If you take supplements, do so with meals to enhance absorption. Some supplements, like fat-soluble vitamins, are better absorbed with food.

As Amritha listened to the story of Priya and the detailed methods for improving nutrient absorption, I could see a new sense of determination in her eyes. She realized that her journey was not just about losing weight, but about nourishing her body in the best possible way.

"Thank you, Dr. Lath," Amritha said, her voice filled with gratitude. "I understand now that it's about more than just eating healthy foods. It's about how I eat them and how my body processes them. I'll start making these changes right away."

With this new knowledge, Amritha's journey took on a deeper meaning. She was not only working towards her weight loss goals but also striving to nourish her body and mind, creating a foundation for lifelong health and well-being.

And so, with renewed motivation and a better understanding of her body's needs, Amritha continued her journey, knowing that each small step was bringing her closer to her ultimate goal.

CHAPTER FIFTEEN

THE CRUCIAL ROLE OF MENTAL PEACE AND A STRESS-FREE LIFE IN WEIGHT MANAGEMENT

Amritha's journey was not just about changing her diet and exercise habits. It was also about addressing the mental and emotional aspects of her life that were affecting her weight. The connection between stress, mental peace, and weight management is profound and scientifically backed, involving a complex interplay of hormones and behaviors.

The Unexpected Stressor

Amritha had been making steady progress. She had adhered to the dietary changes and embraced a more active lifestyle. However, despite her efforts, there were weeks when her weight loss plateaued or she even gained a few pounds. During one of our sessions, I noticed she seemed more tense and anxious than usual.

"Amritha, is everything okay?" I asked gently.

She sighed deeply, her eyes welling up with tears. "Dr. Lath, I feel overwhelmed. My job is demanding, my personal life is chaotic, and I'm constantly stressed. I try to follow the plan, but sometimes I just feel too exhausted mentally to keep up."

I realized then that we needed to address the mental and emotional aspects of her weight loss journey. It wasn't just about what she ate or how much she exercised, but also about her overall mental well-being.

The Impact of Stress on Weight Management

Stress affects the body in numerous ways, particularly in relation to weight management. Here are some of the scientific causes of stress and weight gain:

1. **Hormonal Imbalance:**

- **Cortisol:** Known as the stress hormone, cortisol is released during periods of stress. High levels of cortisol can lead to increased appetite and cravings for high-calorie foods, contributing to weight gain.

- **Insulin:** Chronic stress can lead to insulin resistance, where the body's cells don't respond properly to insulin. This can result in higher blood sugar levels and increased fat storage.

2. **Emotional Eating:**

- Many people turn to food for comfort when they are stressed, leading to overeating and the consumption of unhealthy foods.

3. **Sleep Disruption:**

- Stress can disrupt sleep patterns, leading to poor-quality sleep or insomnia. Lack of sleep affects hormones that regulate hunger, such as ghrelin and leptin, which can increase appetite and cravings for unhealthy foods.

4. **Metabolic Changes:**

- Chronic stress can alter the body's metabolism, making it harder to lose weight and easier to gain it.

5. **Reduced Physical Activity:**

- Stress often leads to fatigue and lack of motivation, reducing the likelihood of engaging in physical activities.

Amritha's Story: Finding Peace Amidst Chaos

One day, after another stressful week at work, Amritha decided to take a walk in a nearby park. The fresh air and natural surroundings provided a much-needed break from her daily grind. As she strolled, she noticed an elderly woman sitting on a bench, knitting peacefully.

Amritha struck up a conversation with the woman, whose name was Lakshmi. She learned that Lakshmi had faced numerous hardships in her life but had always found solace in simple pleasures like knitting, gardening, and spending time in nature.

"Life can be overwhelming," Lakshmi said, her eyes twinkling with wisdom. "But finding peace within yourself is the key. Stress and worry won't change anything, but a calm mind can help you see things clearly and make better decisions."

Amritha left the park that day feeling inspired. She realized she needed to incorporate more moments of peace and relaxation into her life. She started by dedicating time each day to activities that calmed her mind and brought her joy.

Strategies for Reducing Stress and Enhancing Mental Peace

1. **Mindfulness and Meditation:**
- Practicing mindfulness and meditation can help reduce stress levels and promote mental clarity. Even a few minutes a day can make a significant difference.
2. **Regular Physical Activity:**
- Exercise is a natural stress reliever. Activities like yoga, walking, and swimming can help reduce cortisol levels and improve mood.
3. **Adequate Sleep:**
- Prioritizing good sleep hygiene is crucial. Aim for 7-9 hours of quality sleep each night to help regulate hunger hormones and reduce stress.
4. **Healthy Social Connections:**
- Spending time with loved ones and engaging in social activities can provide emotional support and reduce stress.
5. **Hobbies and Leisure Activities:**
- Engaging in hobbies and activities that bring joy can help distract from stress and provide a sense of fulfillment.
6. **Balanced Work-Life Schedule:**
- Maintaining a healthy balance between work and personal life is essential. Setting boundaries and making time for relaxation can help manage stress levels.
7. **Professional Help:**
- Sometimes, talking to a therapist or counselor can provide valuable strategies for managing stress and improving mental health.

Applying These Lessons

Amritha began incorporating these strategies into her daily routine. She started practicing mindfulness meditation every morning, set aside time for her favorite hobbies, and made a conscious effort to get enough sleep. She also learned to say no to extra work commitments that added unnecessary stress.

Gradually, Amritha noticed a change. Not only did she feel more relaxed and happier, but her weight loss progress resumed. Her cravings for unhealthy foods decreased, and she had more energy to stick to her exercise routine.

Summary: The Power of Mental Peace

Mental peace and a stress-free life play a crucial role in managing weight. Stress can lead to hormonal imbalances, emotional eating, sleep disruption, and reduced physical activity, all of which can hinder weight loss efforts. By incorporating stress-reduction strategies such as mindfulness, regular exercise, adequate sleep, healthy social connections, hobbies, and professional help, individuals can enhance their mental well-being and support their weight management goals.

Amritha's journey underscored the importance of addressing both the physical and mental aspects of weight loss. By finding ways to reduce stress and promote mental peace, she was able to overcome obstacles and continue her path towards a healthier and happier life.

CHAPTER SIXTEEN

Understanding the Components of Food: Carbohydrates, Proteins, Fats, Vitamins, Minerals, and Fiber

In this chapter, we will explore the different components of food, their types, their roles in the body, common public perceptions and myths about them, and the best ways to consume these nutrients to lose weight and stay healthy. We will also discuss the importance of fiber.

Components of Food
1. **Carbohydrates**
2. **Proteins**
3. **Fats**
4. **Vitamins**
5. **Minerals**
6. **Fiber**

---

1. Carbohydrates
Types of Carbohydrates:
- **Simple Carbohydrates**: Sugars (glucose, fructose, sucrose)
- **Complex Carbohydrates**: Starches (grains, legumes, potatoes)
- **Fiber**: Indigestible part of plant foods
Role in the Body:
- Provide energy (main source)
- Store energy (glycogen in muscles and liver)
- Spare protein for muscle building and repair
Public Perception and Myths:
- **Myth**: All carbohydrates are bad for weight loss.
- **Reality**: Complex carbohydrates and fiber are essential for a balanced diet. Simple carbohydrates should be limited.
Foods Containing Carbohydrates:
- Simple Carbohydrates: Fruits, sugar, honey, milk
- Complex Carbohydrates: Whole grains (brown rice, whole wheat), legumes, vegetables
- Fiber: Fruits, vegetables, whole grains, legumes

Best Method and Foods to Consume for Weight Loss:

- Focus on whole grains, vegetables, and fruits.

- Avoid refined sugars and processed foods.

- Incorporate fiber-rich foods to promote satiety and digestion.

---

2. Proteins

Types of Proteins:

- **Complete Proteins**: Contain all essential amino acids (animal sources)

- **Incomplete Proteins**: Lack some essential amino acids (plant sources)

Role in the Body:

- Build and repair tissues

- Produce enzymes and hormones

- Support immune function

Public Perception and Myths:

- **Myth**: High-protein diets are always the best for weight loss.

- **Reality**: While protein is crucial for muscle maintenance and satiety, balance with other nutrients is essential.

Foods Containing Proteins:

- Animal Sources: Meat, poultry, fish, eggs, dairy

- Plant Sources: Legumes, nuts, seeds, tofu, quinoa

Best Method and Foods to Consume for Weight Loss:

- Include lean proteins (chicken, fish, beans) in meals.

- Combine plant proteins to ensure all essential amino acids (e.g., rice and beans).

---

3. Fats

Types of Fats:
- **Saturated Fats**: Solid at room temperature (animal fats, butter)
- **Unsaturated Fats**: Liquid at room temperature (olive oil, nuts, seeds)
- **Monounsaturated Fats**
- **Polyunsaturated Fats (including Omega-3 and Omega-6 fatty acids)**
- **Trans Fats**: Industrially produced (partially hydrogenated oils)
Role in the Body:
- Provide long-term energy
- Protect organs
- Aid in absorption of fat-soluble vitamins (A, D, E, K)
- Essential for cell structure and function
Public Perception and Myths:
- **Myth**: All fats are bad and should be avoided.
- **Reality**: Healthy fats are essential for body functions and can aid in weight management.
Foods Containing Fats:
- Saturated Fats: Red meat, butter, cheese
- Unsaturated Fats: Olive oil, avocados, nuts, seeds, fatty fish (salmon, mackerel)
- Trans Fats: Processed foods, baked goods, margarine
Best Method and Foods to Consume for Weight Loss:
- Focus on unsaturated fats, especially from plant sources.
- Limit intake of saturated fats and avoid trans fats.
- Incorporate sources of Omega-3 fatty acids (flaxseeds, chia seeds, fish).

---

4. Vitamins

Types of Vitamins:
- **Water-Soluble Vitamins**: B-complex vitamins, Vitamin C
- **Fat-Soluble Vitamins**: Vitamins A, D, E, K
Role in the Body:
- Support immune function
- Promote bone health
- Assist in energy production
- Act as antioxidants
Public Perception and Myths:
- **Myth**: More vitamins mean better health.
- **Reality**: Vitamins are crucial but need to be balanced. Excessive intake, especially of fat-soluble vitamins, can be harmful.
Foods Containing Vitamins:
- Water-Soluble: Fruits (oranges, strawberries), vegetables (broccoli, bell peppers), whole grains, lean meats
- Fat-Soluble: Leafy greens, fish oils, dairy products, nuts
Best Method and Foods to Consume for Weight Loss:
- Eat a variety of colorful fruits and vegetables.
- Include sources of fat to aid in the absorption of fat-soluble vitamins.
- Avoid relying on supplements unless advised by a healthcare professional.

---

5. Minerals
Types of Minerals:
- **Major Minerals**: Calcium, potassium, sodium, magnesium
- **Trace Minerals**: Iron, zinc, copper, selenium
Role in the Body:

- Support bone health
- Maintain fluid balance
- Aid in nerve transmission
- Support muscle function
Public Perception and Myths:
- **Myth**: Only calcium and iron are important.
- **Reality**: All minerals are essential for various bodily functions.
Foods Containing Minerals:
- Calcium: Dairy products, leafy greens, fortified plant milk
- Potassium: Bananas, potatoes, spinach
- Iron: Red meat, legumes, fortified cereals
- Magnesium: Nuts, seeds, whole grains
Best Method and Foods to Consume for Weight Loss:
- Incorporate a variety of whole foods.
- Choose natural sources over supplements.
- Ensure balanced intake to prevent deficiencies.

---

6. Fiber
Types of Fiber:
- **Soluble Fiber**: Dissolves in water (oats, apples, citrus fruits)
- **Insoluble Fiber**: Does not dissolve in water (whole grains, nuts, vegetables)
Role in the Body:
- Promotes digestive health
- Regulates blood sugar levels
- Lowers cholesterol levels
- Aids in weight management by promoting satiety
Public Perception and Myths:
- **Myth**: Fiber is only important for digestive health.

- **Reality**: Fiber has multiple benefits, including blood sugar control and heart health.
Foods Containing Fiber:
- Soluble Fiber: Oats, apples, beans, carrots
- Insoluble Fiber: Whole wheat bread, brown rice, nuts, cauliflower
Best Method and Foods to Consume for Weight Loss:
- Aim for a mix of soluble and insoluble fiber.
- Include fiber-rich foods like fruits, vegetables, whole grains, and legumes.
- Drink plenty of water to help fiber move through the digestive system.

Summary: Achieving a Balanced Diet
Achieving and maintaining a healthy weight is not about eliminating entire food groups but about understanding and balancing the different components of food. Incorporate a variety of nutrient-dense foods, prioritize whole grains, lean proteins, healthy fats, and fiber-rich foods, and stay hydrated. By doing so, you can ensure your body receives the essential nutrients it needs while managing your weight effectively.

Amritha's Story: The Journey to Balanced Nutrition
In one of our sessions, I explained the importance of a balanced diet to Amritha. She had been avoiding carbohydrates entirely due to the misconception that all carbs were bad for weight loss. After understanding the different types of carbohydrates and their roles, she started including whole grains and fiber-rich vegetables in her diet.

Amritha also realized she had been skimping on healthy fats due to fear of gaining weight. Learning about the benefits of unsaturated fats, she began incorporating nuts, seeds, and olive oil into her meals.

Gradually, Amritha's energy levels improved, her digestive health benefited from the increased fiber intake, and she felt more satisfied with her meals, which helped her stay on track with her weight loss goals. This balanced approach not only helped her lose weight but also improved her overall health and well-being.

CATEGORIES OF FOOD ACCORDING TO CALORIES:

A calorie is a unit of energy that measures how much energy food provides to your body. When you eat food, your body uses calories for various activities, from breathing to running. If you consume more calories than your body needs, the extra calories are stored as fat, leading to weight gain. Conversely, if you consume fewer calories than your body needs, your body will use stored fat for energy, resulting in weight loss. Therefore, managing calorie intake is crucial for controlling your weight.

Here is a table with the four categories of food, suitable examples of Indian food in each category, and an explanation of which foods are better for us and why.

Category*

<u>Low Calorie, Low Volume</u>

- Foods that are low in calories and small in portion
- Papaya, Cucumber Slices, Spinach Salad
- These foods are generally better for weight loss as they provide essential nutrients without adding many

calories. They are ideal for controlling calorie intake.

Low Calorie, High Volume

- Foods that are low in calories but larger in portion |
- Watermelon, Salad with lots of vegetables, Soup
- These foods are beneficial because they fill you up without adding many calories. They can help you feel full and satisfied, reducing the likelihood of overeating.

High Calorie, High Volume

- Foods that are high in calories and large in portion
- Butter Chicken, Biryani, Samosas
- These foods should be consumed in moderation as they provide a lot of calories in large portions, which can lead to weight gain if eaten frequently.

High Calorie, Low Volume

- Foods that are high in calories but small in portion |
- Gulab Jamun, Cashew Nuts, Ghee
- These foods are very dense in calories, so even small portions can add a significant amount of calories. They should be limited to avoid excessive calorie intake
-

Which Foods are Better for Us and Why

1. **Low Calorie, High Volume Foods**: These are generally the best for maintaining a healthy diet. They help you feel full and satisfied without consuming too many calories. Examples include watermelon and salads with lots

of vegetables. These foods are rich in water and fiber, which are beneficial for digestion and overall health.

2. **Low Calorie, Low Volume Foods**: While also good for weight management, these foods might not be as filling as their high-volume counterparts. However, they are still beneficial due to their low-calorie content and nutrient density. Examples include papaya and cucumber slices.

3. **High Calorie, High Volume Foods**: These should be consumed in moderation. Although they can be part of a balanced diet, their high calorie content can contribute to weight gain if eaten frequently. Examples include butter chicken and biryani.

4. **High Calorie, Low Volume Foods**: These should be eaten sparingly as they are very calorie-dense and can easily lead to excessive calorie intake even in small portions. Examples include gulab jamun and ghee.

By focusing on low-calorie, high-volume foods, you can create a diet that is both satisfying and conducive to weight management, ensuring you get enough nutrients without excessive calorie intake.

CHAPTER SEVENTEEN

UNDERSTANDING GLYCEMIC INDEX AND GLYCEMIC LOAD

In this chapter, we will explore the concepts of Glycemic Index (GI) and Glycemic Load (GL), their importance in weight loss, and how knowledge of these can help in selecting healthier food options. We will also provide suitable examples of common Indian foods to illustrate these concepts.

Glycemic Index (GI)
Definition:
The Glycemic Index is a measure that ranks carbohydrates in foods according to their impact on blood sugar levels. Foods are scored on a scale of 0 to 100, with pure glucose given a value of 100.

Categories:

- **Low GI (55 or less)**: Foods that cause a slow, gradual rise in blood sugar.
- **Medium GI (56-69)**: Foods that cause a moderate rise in blood sugar.
- **High GI (70 or more)**: Foods that cause a rapid spike in blood sugar.

Importance in Weight Loss:

- **Satiety**: Low GI foods help maintain a feeling of fullness, reducing overall calorie intake.
- **Blood Sugar Control**: Consuming low GI foods helps in managing blood sugar levels, which can prevent insulin spikes and reduce the risk of type 2 diabetes.
- **Sustained Energy**: Low GI foods provide a steady supply of energy, preventing energy crashes and cravings for unhealthy snacks.

Examples of Indian Foods by GI:

- **Low GI**: Lentils (dal), chickpeas (chana), vegetables (spinach, cauliflower), whole grains (brown rice, barley)
- **Medium GI**: Basmati rice, sweet potatoes, whole wheat chapati
- **High GI**: White rice, potatoes, white bread, puffed rice

---

Glycemic Load (GL)

Definition:

The Glycemic Load is a measure that takes into account the GI of a food and the amount of carbohydrate it contains in a serving. It provides a more accurate picture of how a food will affect blood sugar levels.

Calculation:

GL = (GI x Carbohydrate content in grams per serving) / 100

Categories:
- **Low GL (10 or less)**: Indicates a smaller impact on blood sugar levels.
- **Medium GL (11-19)**: Indicates a moderate impact on blood sugar levels.
- **High GL (20 or more)**: Indicates a significant impact on blood sugar levels.

Importance in Weight Loss:
- **Balanced Blood Sugar**: Managing GL helps in keeping blood sugar levels stable, aiding in better weight management.
- **Portion Control**: Understanding GL helps in choosing appropriate portion sizes, ensuring that even higher GI foods can be consumed in moderation without causing significant blood sugar spikes.
- **Dietary Choices**: Helps in making informed decisions about which foods to include in the diet for optimal health and weight loss.

Examples of Indian Foods by GL:
- **Low GL**: Dal (lentils), mixed vegetable curry, small serving of brown rice
- **Medium GL**: Moderate serving of basmati rice, roti with sabzi
- **High GL**: Large serving of white rice, potatoes, sugary sweets

---

Importance of GI and GL in Selecting Foods for Weight Loss

Understanding GI and GL:
- **GI and GL Help with Food Selection**: By choosing foods with low to medium GI and GL, you can create a diet that promotes stable blood sugar levels, increases satiety, and provides sustained energy.

- **Prevent Overeating**: Low GI and GL foods help control hunger and reduce cravings, preventing overeating and aiding in weight loss.

- **Balanced Diet**: Knowledge of GI and GL encourages the inclusion of a variety of nutrient-dense foods, promoting a balanced and healthy diet.

Practical Tips for Indian Diet:

1. **Opt for Whole Grains**: Replace white rice with brown rice or millets. Use whole wheat for chapatis instead of refined flour.

2. **Include Legumes**: Add lentils, chickpeas, and beans to meals for protein and fiber.

3. **Eat More Vegetables**: Fill half your plate with non-starchy vegetables to lower the overall GI of your meal.

4. **Limit Sugary Foods**: Avoid sweets and sugary snacks. Opt for fruits like apples or berries for a sweet treat with a lower GI.

5. **Combine Foods**: Pair high GI foods with low GI foods to balance the overall GI of the meal. For example, eat white rice with a large portion of vegetables and some dal.

Examples of Balanced Indian Meals Based on GI and GL

1. **Breakfast**:

- **Low GI**: Oats porridge with nuts and a small portion of fruit (like an apple).

- **Medium GI**: Poha with lots of vegetables and a squeeze of lemon.

2. **Lunch**:

- **Low GI**: Brown rice with mixed vegetable curry and a side of dal.

- **Medium GI**: Basmati rice with chicken curry and a cucumber salad.

3. **Dinner**:

- **Low GI**: Whole wheat chapati with palak paneer and a bowl of dal.

- **Medium GI**: Roti with grilled fish and sautéed vegetables.

4. **Snacks**:

- **Low GI**: Carrot sticks with hummus, a handful of almonds.

- **Medium GI**: Boiled chickpeas (chana) chaat with lemon and spices.

Conclusion

Understanding the Glycemic Index and Glycemic Load of foods can significantly enhance your ability to choose foods that support weight loss and overall health. By incorporating low to medium GI and GL foods into your diet, you can maintain stable blood sugar levels, feel fuller for longer, and prevent overeating. This knowledge allows for better dietary choices, contributing to a balanced and sustainable weight management plan.

CHAPTER EIGHTEEN

THE ROLE OF PROTEIN IN OUR BODY

In this chapter, we delve into the significance of protein in our body, its various functions, and why it's essential for overall health and well-being.

Understanding Protein
Definition:
Proteins are macronutrients made up of amino acids, often referred to as the building blocks of life. They play a crucial role in various bodily functions and are necessary for the growth, repair, and maintenance of tissues.
Types of Proteins:
- **Complete Proteins**: Contain all essential amino acids. Found in animal sources like meat, poultry, fish, eggs, and dairy.
- **Incomplete Proteins**: Lack one or more essential amino acids. Found in plant sources like legumes, nuts, seeds, and grains.

Role in the Body:

1. **Muscle Building and Repair**: Proteins are vital for building and repairing muscle tissues. They provide the necessary amino acids needed for muscle growth and recovery after exercise or injury.

2. **Enzyme Production**: Enzymes are proteins that facilitate biochemical reactions in the body, such as digestion, metabolism, and cellular processes.

3. **Hormone Regulation**: Certain proteins act as hormones, regulating various physiological processes like growth, metabolism, and reproduction.

4. **Immune Function**: Proteins play a crucial role in immune function by producing antibodies that help fight off infections and diseases.

5. **Transportation and Storage**: Proteins transport essential molecules like oxygen (hemoglobin) and nutrients (albumin) throughout the body. They also store certain nutrients for future use.

Importance of Protein in Weight Loss:

- **Muscle Preservation**: Adequate protein intake during weight loss helps preserve lean muscle mass, ensuring that the body primarily burns fat for energy.

- **Satiety**: Protein-rich foods promote feelings of fullness and satiety, reducing overall calorie intake and preventing overeating.

- **Thermic Effect**: Protein has a higher thermic effect compared to carbohydrates and fats, meaning it requires more energy to digest and metabolize, leading to increased calorie expenditure.

- **Metabolic Rate**: Protein metabolism increases metabolic rate, helping to burn more calories at rest.

Common Myths about Protein:

1. **Myth**: High-protein diets are harmful to kidney health.
   - **Reality**: While excessive protein intake may strain the kidneys in individuals with pre-existing kidney conditions, moderate protein consumption is safe for most people.
2. **Myth**: Plant-based proteins are inferior to animal-based proteins.
   - **Reality**: Plant-based proteins can provide all essential amino acids when consumed in adequate amounts and complemented with a varied diet.

Best Sources of Protein:

1. **Animal Sources**: Meat, poultry, fish, eggs, dairy products (milk, yogurt, cheese)
2. **Plant Sources**: Legumes (beans, lentils, chickpeas), nuts, seeds, tofu, tempeh, quinoa, seitan

Recommended Protein Intake:

- The Recommended Dietary Allowance (RDA) for protein is approximately 0.8 grams per kilogram of body weight for adults. However, individual protein needs may vary based on factors such as age, gender, activity level, and health status.

Practical Tips for Including Protein in Your Diet

1. **Prioritize Protein at Every Meal**: Include a source of protein (animal or plant-based) in each meal to ensure adequate intake throughout the day.
2. **Choose Lean Protein Sources**: Opt for lean cuts of meat, skinless poultry, fish, and low-fat dairy to minimize saturated fat intake.
3. **Diversify Protein Sources**: Incorporate a variety of protein-rich foods into your diet to obtain a wide range

of essential amino acids.

4. **Snack on Protein**: Enjoy protein-rich snacks like Greek yogurt, cottage cheese, hard-boiled eggs, or nuts to curb hunger between meals.

5. **Consider Protein Supplements**: If struggling to meet protein needs through whole foods alone, protein supplements like whey protein powder, pea protein, or soy protein can be convenient options.

Conclusion

Protein is a fundamental nutrient that plays a vital role in various physiological functions in the body. Whether you're looking to build muscle, lose weight, or maintain overall health, adequate protein intake is essential. By understanding the importance of protein, incorporating protein-rich foods into your diet, and debunking common myths, you can optimize your nutritional intake and support your health and fitness goals effectively.

CHAPTER NINETEEN

THE RISE OF EXCLUSIVE PROTEIN SHAKES FOR WEIGHT LOSS

In recent years, exclusive protein shakes have gained immense popularity among youngsters as a quick-fix solution for weight loss. These shakes promise rapid results, enticing consumers with the allure of a leaner, fitter physique in a short amount of time. However, behind the glossy marketing lies a complex landscape of pros and cons, along with significant financial costs. In this chapter, we delve into the world of exclusive protein shakes, exploring their benefits and drawbacks, and unraveling the human story of Riya, a young woman whose journey with these shakes took a toll on her health and well-being.

The Allure of Exclusive Protein Shakes
Exclusive protein shakes have become synonymous with modern weight loss culture, offering a convenient and

seemingly effective way to shed unwanted pounds. Marketed as meal replacements or supplements, these shakes typically contain high levels of protein, minimal carbohydrates and fats, and a range of added vitamins and minerals. The appeal lies in their simplicity – a quick shake in place of a meal, promising to keep hunger at bay while promoting muscle growth and fat loss.

The Pros of Exclusive Protein Shakes

1. **Convenience**: For busy individuals, protein shakes offer a convenient and time-saving option for meal replacement. With hectic schedules and on-the-go lifestyles, many find it easier to grab a shake than to prepare a balanced meal.

2. **Muscle Maintenance**: Protein is essential for muscle repair and growth. By consuming protein shakes, especially after workouts, individuals can support muscle recovery and prevent muscle loss during weight loss efforts.

3. **Portion Control**: Protein shakes provide a controlled portion size, eliminating the need for calorie counting or portion measuring. This simplicity can be appealing for those seeking structure in their diet.

The Cons of Exclusive Protein Shakes

1. **Nutritional Deficiencies**: Despite their protein content, exclusive protein shakes often lack essential nutrients found in whole foods, such as fiber, vitamins, and minerals. Relying solely on shakes for nutrition can lead to deficiencies and imbalances in the diet.

2. **Digestive Issues**: Some individuals may experience digestive discomfort, bloating, or constipation when consuming high levels of protein in liquid form. This can be exacerbated by artificial additives or sweeteners commonly found in protein shakes.

3. **Long-Term Sustainability**: While protein shakes may yield short-term weight loss results, they are not sustainable as a long-term dietary strategy. Without education on healthy eating habits and portion control, individuals may struggle to maintain weight loss once they resume regular eating patterns.

4. **Financial Costs**: The cost of purchasing exclusive protein shakes can be prohibitive for many individuals, especially considering the ongoing nature of weight loss efforts. Additionally, some may find it difficult to afford these shakes as a regular dietary expense.

Riya's Story: A Journey of Struggle and Redemption

Riya, a 25-year-old marketing executive, was determined to lose weight and sculpt her body into a leaner, more toned version of herself. Influenced by social media influencers and celebrity endorsements, she embarked on a journey with exclusive protein shakes, believing they held the key to her dream physique.

At first, Riya was thrilled with the initial results. The pounds seemed to melt away, and she reveled in the compliments from friends and colleagues. However, as weeks turned into months, Riya began to notice alarming changes in her health. She experienced constant fatigue, hair loss, and muscle weakness, despite adhering strictly to her protein shake regimen.

Concerned about her declining health, Riya sought the advice of a nutritionist, who diagnosed her with nutritional deficiencies stemming from her exclusive reliance on protein shakes. Shocked and disheartened, Riya realized the toll that her pursuit of an idealized body had taken on her physical and emotional well-being.

With guidance from her healthcare provider, Riya gradually transitioned away from exclusive protein shakes and embraced a balanced diet rich in whole foods. It wasn't easy – there were setbacks and moments of doubt – but Riya was determined to reclaim her health and happiness. Slowly but surely, she regained the weight she had lost and, more importantly, rediscovered her vitality and zest for life.

Today, Riya serves as a cautionary tale, a reminder that true health and wellness cannot be achieved through shortcuts or quick fixes. Her journey serves as an inspiration to others, urging them to prioritize their well-being over societal pressures and unrealistic standards of beauty.

The Cost of Pursuing Perfection

Riya's story is a poignant reminder of the hidden costs associated with the pursuit of perfection. While exclusive protein shakes may promise the allure of a slimmer physique, the toll on one's health – both physical and emotional – can be immeasurable. As Riya discovered, the price of prioritizing aesthetics over well-being is simply too high to pay.

In the end, the true measure of success lies not in the number on the scale or the reflection in the mirror, but in the ability to nourish and honor the body from within. Riya's journey serves as a powerful testament to the resilience of the human spirit and the transformative power of self-love and self-acceptance.

Conclusion: Navigating the Complex Terrain of Exclusive Protein Shakes

Exclusive protein shakes may offer a tempting shortcut to weight loss, but their benefits must be weighed against their potential risks and limitations. While convenient and potentially effective in the short term, these shakes are not a sustainable solution for long-term health and wellness. Riya's story serves as a poignant reminder of the importance of balance, moderation, and self-care in our journey toward a healthier, happier life. As we navigate the complex terrain of diet culture and body image ideals, may we strive to prioritize our well-being above all else, embracing the beauty of imperfection and the power of self-love along the way.

UNDERSTANDING FAT - AMRITHA'S JOURNEY TO OVERCOMING THE FEAR OF FAT

Fat. For many, this three-letter word is synonymous with guilt, indulgence, and the fear of weight gain. Yet, fat is an essential macronutrient that plays crucial roles in our body, from supporting cell structure to providing energy. This chapter aims to dispel myths, offer clarity on the types of fat, and guide you on how to incorporate fats healthily into your diet. As we explore these facets, we'll weave in the emotional story of Amritha, a young woman whose struggle with fat shaped her journey toward a healthier, happier self.

What is Fat and Its Role in the Body?
Definition:

Fats, also known as lipids, are organic compounds made up of carbon, hydrogen, and oxygen. They are one of the three primary macronutrients, along with carbohydrates and proteins, essential for the body's overall function and well-being.

Roles of Fat in the Body:

1. **Energy Source:** Fats are a concentrated source of energy, providing 9 calories per gram, more than twice that of carbohydrates and proteins. They serve as a long-term energy reserve, especially important during periods of fasting or low food intake.

2. **Cell Structure:** Fat is a key component of cell membranes, helping to maintain their structure and fluidity. This is vital for the proper functioning of cells and the communication between them.

3. **Insulation and Protection:** Fats provide insulation to help maintain body temperature and protect vital organs by cushioning them against shock and injury.

4. **Nutrient Absorption:** Certain vitamins, such as A, D, E, and K, are fat-soluble, meaning they require dietary fat for proper absorption and utilization by the body.

5. **Hormone Production:** Fats are involved in the production of essential hormones, including sex hormones like estrogen and testosterone, which regulate various physiological processes.

6. **Flavor and Satiety:** Fat enhances the flavor of foods and provides a feeling of satiety, helping to control hunger and prevent overeating.

Myths Associated with Fats

1. **Myth: Eating Fat Makes You Fat.**
- **Reality:** While excess calorie intake, regardless of the source, can lead to weight gain, not all fats are created equal. Healthy fats, when consumed in moderation, do not

directly cause weight gain and can be part of a balanced diet.

2. **Myth: All Fats are Unhealthy.**

- **Reality:** There are different types of fats, some of which are essential for health. Unsaturated fats, particularly monounsaturated (MUFA) and polyunsaturated fats (PUFA), are beneficial and support various bodily functions.

3. **Myth: Low-Fat Diets are Best for Weight Loss.**

- **Reality:** Extremely low-fat diets can lead to deficiencies in essential fatty acids and fat-soluble vitamins. A balanced approach that includes healthy fats is more sustainable and beneficial for long-term health.

4. **Myth: Saturated Fats Should be Completely Avoided.**

- **Reality:** While it's true that excessive intake of saturated fats can contribute to health issues, moderate consumption, particularly from whole foods like dairy and meat, can be part of a healthy diet.

Amritha's Story: The Struggle with Fat and Self-Worth

Amritha's relationship with fat was deeply intertwined with her self-esteem and her tumultuous marriage. From the outset, her husband had a fixation on her appearance, often criticizing her for her weight. His words were sharp and unkind, slicing through her confidence and leaving her feeling unworthy. The most painful moments were when he would make disparaging comments about her "pot-bellied" appearance in front of others, an experience that left her humiliated and motivated to change.

Amritha vividly recalled one evening when she had prepared a special dinner for their anniversary. She had spent hours in the kitchen, hoping to rekindle the love and warmth in their marriage. Instead, her husband's only remark was about how she should join him in cutting down on the "fatty foods" she had cooked. That night, she cried herself to sleep, vowing to take control of her body and, hopefully, her life.

Her journey to weight loss was not just about shedding pounds but reclaiming her self-worth and silencing the negative voices that had plagued her. As her doctor, I guided her through understanding the real role of fats in her diet, emphasizing that fats are not the enemy but an essential part of a balanced diet.

Classification of Fats

Fats are classified based on their chemical structure and their effects on health. The main types include:

1. **Saturated Fats:**

- **Definition:** These fats have no double bonds between the carbon atoms in their chains. They are typically solid at room temperature.

- **Sources:** Ghee, butter, coconut oil, palm oil, cheese, red meat.

- **Health Impact:** While necessary in small amounts, excessive intake of saturated fats can increase cholesterol levels and the risk of heart disease.

2. **Unsaturated Fats:**

- **Monounsaturated Fats (MUFA):**

- **Definition:** These fats contain one double bond in their structure.

- **Sources:** Olive oil, canola oil, peanut oil, avocados, nuts (almonds, cashews, peanuts).

- **Health Impact:** MUFAs can help reduce bad cholesterol levels and lower the risk of heart disease.

- **Polyunsaturated Fats (PUFA):**

- **Definition:** These fats have more than one double bond in their structure.
- **Sources:** Sunflower oil, soybean oil, corn oil, walnuts, flaxseeds, fatty fish (salmon, mackerel, sardines).
- **Health Impact:** PUFAs, including omega-3 and omega-6 fatty acids, are essential for brain function, inflammation regulation, and heart health.

3. **Trans Fats:**
- **Definition:** These fats are artificially created through hydrogenation, which turns liquid oils into solid fats.
- **Sources:** Partially hydrogenated oils, processed and fried foods, baked goods (cookies, cakes, pastries).
- **Health Impact:** Trans fats are the most harmful, increasing bad cholesterol levels, lowering good cholesterol levels, and raising the risk of heart disease and stroke.

Types of Fatty Acids

1. **Omega-3 Fatty Acids:**
- **Sources:** Fatty fish, flaxseeds, chia seeds, walnuts.
- **Benefits:** Reduce inflammation, support heart health, improve brain function.

2. **Omega-6 Fatty Acids:**
- **Sources:** Vegetable oils (corn oil, soybean oil), nuts, seeds.
- **Benefits:** Essential for growth and development, but must be balanced with omega-3 intake to avoid promoting inflammation.

3. **Omega-9 Fatty Acids:**
- **Sources:** Olive oil, canola oil, sunflower oil, almonds.
- **Benefits:** Help reduce the risk of cardiovascular diseases and improve immune function.

Incorporating Fats into Your Diet

1. **Choose Healthy Fats:** Focus on incorporating more MUFAs and PUFAs into your diet while limiting saturated fats and avoiding trans fats.

2. **Balance Your Fat Intake:** Aim for a balanced intake of omega-3 and omega-6 fatty acids. Prioritize sources like fatty fish, flaxseeds, and walnuts for omega-3s.

3. **Enjoy Moderation:** It's okay to indulge in your favorite fatty foods occasionally. The key is moderation and balance. Enjoy a slice of cake or some fried snacks without guilt, but make it a treat rather than a habit.

4. **Mindful Eating:** Pay attention to portion sizes and avoid mindless eating. Use smaller plates, eat slowly, and savor your meals.

5. **Cook Smart:** Use healthier cooking methods like grilling, steaming, and baking instead of frying. Opt for oils high in unsaturated fats, such as olive oil or canola oil.

6. **Snack Wisely:** Choose healthy snacks like nuts, seeds, and avocado slices over processed snacks and fried foods.

Riya's Relapse and Realization

One particularly challenging period for Amritha was when she tried an extreme low-fat diet, influenced by misinformation and societal pressure. Her husband's criticism about her "pot-bellied" appearance had deeply affected her, pushing her to eliminate almost all fats from her diet in an attempt to lose weight quickly.

Initially, Amritha saw some results, but soon her energy levels plummeted, and she felt constantly fatigued and irritable. Her skin lost its luster, and she experienced hair loss. More alarmingly, she started having irregular menstrual cycles. It was then that she realized that her approach was not sustainable or healthy.

With guidance, Amritha reintroduced healthy fats into her diet, focusing on balance and moderation. She learned that fats were not her enemy but a vital part of her nutrition. She started incorporating foods rich in MUFAs and PUFAs, such as avocados, nuts, seeds, and olive oil. Gradually, her energy levels improved, her skin regained its glow, and her overall health stabilized.

Through this journey, Amritha also worked on her emotional health. She realized that her self-worth was not defined by her weight or her husband's harsh words. She started practicing self-compassion and surrounded herself with supportive friends who encouraged her to embrace a holistic approach to health and well-being.

Amritha's Empowering Discovery

One turning point for Amritha was when she attended a nutrition workshop. Here, she learned about the different types of fats and their roles in the body. She discovered that fats were not just about calories but were crucial for her overall health. This knowledge empowered her to make informed choices and not be swayed by societal pressures or marketing gimmicks.

She began incorporating a variety of healthy fats into her meals. Breakfast often included avocado toast or a handful of nuts. She used olive oil in her cooking and enjoyed salmon and other fatty fish rich in omega-3s. These changes not only helped her feel satiated but also improved her mood and energy levels.

Selecting Fats for Weight Loss and Health

1. **Embrace Variety:** Include a variety of fat sources in your diet to ensure you get a balance of different fatty acids. Mix and match MUFAs, PUFAs, and small amounts of saturated fats from whole foods.

2. **Read Labels:** Be mindful of food labels and ingredients. Avoid products with trans fats or partially hydrogenated oils.

3. **Limit Processed Foods:** Processed and fried foods often contain unhealthy fats. Opt for whole, unprocessed foods whenever possible.

4. **Healthy Snacking:** Choose snacks like almonds, walnuts, or yogurt with a drizzle of honey and seeds over chips or sugary treats.

5. **Cooking Methods:** Use healthier cooking methods like grilling, steaming, or baking. When frying, use oils high in unsaturated fats and avoid reusing oil.

Conclusion: Embracing Healthy Fats and Self-Love

Amritha's journey underscores the importance of understanding the role of fats in our diet and dispelling common myths. Fats are not the enemy; they are a vital component of a healthy diet that supports overall well-being. By embracing healthy fats and adopting a balanced approach, Amritha found a sustainable path to health and happiness.

Her story also highlights the emotional aspects of weight loss and body image. Criticism and societal pressure can deeply affect self-esteem, but knowledge and self-compassion can empower individuals to make healthier choices. Amritha's journey from fear and misinformation to understanding and balance serves as an inspiring reminder that true health is about nurturing both the body and the mind.

Incorporating healthy fats into our diets, choosing variety and moderation, and focusing on overall well-being rather than just weight loss can lead to a healthier, happier life. As Amritha discovered, it's not about eliminating fats but about understanding their role and making informed, balanced choices that support long-term health and vitality.

Fats vs. Fatty Acids: A Simple Explanation

Fats:

- **Definition:** Fats are a type of nutrient found in food that your body uses for energy, insulation, and cell function.

- **Form:** Fats are typically found in foods in the form of triglycerides, which consist of three fatty acids attached to a glycerol backbone.

- **Sources:** Common sources include butter, oils, nuts, meat, and dairy products.

Fatty Acids:

- **Definition:** Fatty acids are the building blocks of fats. They are long chains of carbon atoms bonded to hydrogen atoms.

- **Types:** There are different types of fatty acids, such as saturated, monounsaturated, and polyunsaturated, which differ based on their chemical structure.

- **Role:** Fatty acids can be used by the body directly for energy or stored as fat. They are also essential for building cell membranes and producing hormones.

Key Difference:

- **Fats** are the whole nutrient we consume, which our body breaks down into **fatty acids** during digestion. Think of fats as the complete structure (like a car), while fatty acids are the individual parts (like the engine, wheels, and seats) that make up the car.

Understanding Trans Fats

What are Trans Fats?

Trans fats, or trans-fatty acids, are a type of unsaturated fat that occurs in small amounts in nature but is largely a product of industrial processes. These fats are created through a process called hydrogenation, where hydrogen is added to liquid vegetable oils to make them more solid and increase their shelf life. This process is popular in the food industry because it enhances the texture, flavor, and stability of products.

There are two types of trans fats:

1. **Natural Trans Fats:** Found in small quantities in the fat of ruminant animals like cows and sheep. These are present in dairy products and meat.

2. **Artificial Trans Fats:** Produced industrially through hydrogenation. These are found in a wide array of processed foods, including margarine, snack foods, packaged baked goods, and fried foods.

Sources of Trans Fats

Trans fats are pervasive in many processed foods due to their ability to enhance flavor, texture, and shelf life. Some common sources include:

1. **Packaged Baked Goods:** Cookies, cakes, pastries, and pie crusts often contain trans fats.

2. **Snack Foods:** Chips, microwave popcorn, and crackers frequently have trans fats.

3. **Fried Foods:** Doughnuts, fried chicken, French fries, and other deep-fried items are significant sources.

4. **Margarines and Shortenings:** Many stick margarines and vegetable shortenings are high in trans fats.

5. **Frozen Foods:** Some frozen pizzas and frozen dinners contain trans fats.

6. **Cream-Filled Candies:** Many types of chocolate and candies with cream fillings have trans fats.

Health Hazards of Trans Fats

Trans fats are detrimental to health and are associated with numerous health risks. Here are some key hazards:

1. **Heart Disease:**
- Trans fats increase levels of LDL (bad) cholesterol while decreasing HDL (good) cholesterol. This imbalance leads to the buildup of plaque in arteries, increasing the risk of heart disease and stroke.
- Studies have shown a direct link between trans fat consumption and the risk of coronary artery disease. Even small amounts can be harmful.

2. **Inflammation:**
- Trans fats contribute to systemic inflammation, which is a root cause of many chronic diseases, including heart disease, diabetes, and arthritis.

3. **Diabetes:**
- Consumption of trans fats has been linked to insulin resistance, a precursor to diabetes. This means the body becomes less effective at using insulin, leading to higher blood sugar levels.

4. **Obesity:**
- Trans fats are calorie-dense and can contribute to weight gain. They also tend to increase abdominal fat, which is associated with higher health risks than fat stored in other areas.

5. **Cancer:**
- Some studies suggest a potential link between trans fat intake and certain cancers, such as breast and colorectal cancer. However, more research is needed to confirm these associations.

6. **Liver Dysfunction:**
- Trans fats can negatively affect liver function, leading to conditions like fatty liver disease.

7. **Neurodegenerative Diseases:**
- Emerging research indicates that trans fats might play a role in the development of neurodegenerative diseases

such as Alzheimer's disease by contributing to brain inflammation and other damaging processes.

8. **Hormonal Imbalances:**

- Trans fats can disrupt normal hormonal functions, which can impact everything from mood and energy levels to reproductive health.

Identifying Trans Fats in Your Diet

Understanding how to identify and avoid trans fats is crucial for maintaining good health. Here are some tips to help you recognize and steer clear of trans fats:

1. **Read Nutrition Labels:**

- Check the ingredient list on food packages. Look for terms like "partially hydrogenated oils" or "hydrogenated oils," which indicate the presence of trans fats.

- In many countries, food labels are required to list trans fat content. Aim to choose products with 0 grams of trans fat. However, be aware that products containing less than 0.5 grams of trans fat per serving can still be labeled as 0 grams, so it's essential to check the ingredient list as well.

2. **Beware of Fried Foods:**

- Fried foods, especially those from fast-food restaurants, are often high in trans fats. Opt for baked or grilled alternatives whenever possible.

3. **Limit Processed and Packaged Foods:**

- Many processed and packaged foods, such as baked goods, snacks, and convenience foods, contain trans fats. Choose whole, unprocessed foods like fruits, vegetables, whole grains, and lean proteins.

4. **Choose Healthier Fats:**

- Use oils high in unsaturated fats, such as olive oil, avocado oil, and canola oil, for cooking and baking. These fats are healthier alternatives to hydrogenated oils and margarine.

- Incorporate foods rich in omega-3 fatty acids, such as fish, flaxseeds, and walnuts, into your diet.

5. **Homemade Meals:**

- Cooking at home allows you to control the ingredients and avoid trans fats. Use fresh, whole ingredients and avoid processed food products.

Reducing Trans Fats in Your Diet

1. **Cook at Home:**

- Preparing meals at home gives you control over the ingredients and cooking methods. Use healthy oils and avoid pre-packaged mixes that may contain trans fats.

2. **Choose Healthier Alternatives:**

- Replace trans fat-rich foods with healthier alternatives. For example, opt for air-popped popcorn instead of microwave popcorn, and choose whole-grain crackers over processed snacks.

3. **Opt for Natural Fats:**

- Include natural fats in your diet, such as those found in avocados, nuts, seeds, and fatty fish. These fats are beneficial for health and can help reduce the intake of harmful trans fats.

4. **Check Restaurant Menus:**

- When dining out, ask about the types of fats used in cooking. Many restaurants offer healthier options or can modify dishes to reduce trans fat content.

5. **Avoid Processed Foods:**

- Limit your consumption of processed and pre-packaged foods, which are common sources of trans fats. Focus on whole, unprocessed foods to improve your overall diet quality.

The Story of Riya: A Cautionary Tale

Riya was a young woman with a vibrant personality and a zest for life. However, her struggle with weight had always been a source of insecurity. Influenced by glossy advertisements and social media influencers, she decided to embark on a diet that heavily relied on processed foods claiming to be low-fat or fat-free. Little did she know, these foods were often loaded with trans fats.

For months, Riya consumed microwave popcorn, packaged snacks, and fast foods, believing she was making healthier choices by avoiding natural fats. At first, she noticed some weight loss, but soon, the downsides began to appear. She felt constantly tired, her skin lost its glow, and she experienced frequent mood swings. Worse, her cholesterol levels shot up, and her doctor warned her about the risk of heart disease.

Desperate for a solution, Riya sought my advice. Together, we analyzed her diet and identified the culprit: trans fats. We replaced her snacks with whole foods, incorporated healthy fats like avocados and nuts, and focused on home-cooked meals. Gradually, Riya's health improved. She regained her energy, her skin became radiant again, and her cholesterol levels normalized.

Through Riya's story, it's clear that avoiding trans fats is crucial for long-term health. Her journey serves as a reminder that not all fats are bad, and understanding the types of fats we consume can significantly impact our well-being.

Conclusion

Trans fats are harmful to health, contributing to a range of serious health issues from heart disease to inflammation and beyond. Identifying and avoiding trans fats is crucial for maintaining good health. By reading labels, choosing healthier fats, and focusing on whole, unprocessed foods, we can protect ourselves from the dangers of trans fats.

Riya's story is a testament to the importance of being informed about what we eat. Her journey from consuming trans fat-laden foods to embracing a balanced diet rich in healthy fats highlights the positive impact dietary choices can have on our health. As we continue to learn about nutrition, it's essential to remember that not all fats are created equal, and making informed choices can lead to a healthier, happier life.

How to Include Fats in Your Diet to Lose Weight

Including fats in your diet while trying to lose weight can seem counterintuitive, but the right types and amounts of fats can actually help with weight loss. Here's a comprehensive guide on how to incorporate fats effectively to aid in shedding those extra pounds.

Understanding the Right Types of Fats

1. **Monounsaturated Fats (MUFA):**

- **Sources:** Olive oil, avocados, nuts (almonds, cashews, peanuts), seeds (sesame, pumpkin).

- **Benefits:** MUFAs help reduce bad cholesterol levels, lower heart disease risk, and provide essential nutrients to help maintain and develop your body's cells. They also help in regulating blood sugar levels.

- **Inclusion Tips:** Use olive oil for cooking, add avocados to salads, and snack on nuts in moderation.

2. **Polyunsaturated Fats (PUFA):**

- **Sources:** Fatty fish (salmon, mackerel, sardines), flaxseeds, chia seeds, walnuts, soybean oil.

- **Benefits:** PUFAs, especially omega-3 and omega-6 fatty acids, are crucial for brain function and cell growth. Omega-3s are known to reduce inflammation and may lower the risk of heart disease, cancer, and arthritis.

- **Inclusion Tips:** Include fatty fish in your meals twice a week, sprinkle flaxseeds or chia seeds on yogurt or salads, and use soybean oil in cooking.

3. **Saturated Fats:**

- **Sources:** Butter, cheese, red meat, coconut oil.

- **Benefits:** While traditionally viewed negatively, moderate amounts of saturated fats can be part of a balanced diet. They help with hormone production and absorption of fat-soluble vitamins.

- **Inclusion Tips:** Limit intake to about 10% of your daily calories. Opt for lean cuts of meat and use butter sparingly.

4. **Trans Fats:**

- **Sources:** Processed foods, margarine, fried foods, baked goods.

- **Risks:** Trans fats increase bad cholesterol levels and lower good cholesterol levels, contributing to a higher risk of heart disease and other health problems.

- **Inclusion Tips:** Avoid trans fats as much as possible by reading labels and steering clear of processed foods.

Timing and Portion Control

1. **Timing of Fat Intake:**

- **Morning:** Starting your day with a healthy fat can provide sustained energy. Incorporate fats into your breakfast by adding avocado to your toast, sprinkling chia seeds into your smoothie, or cooking eggs in olive oil.

- **Midday:** A balanced lunch with healthy fats can help maintain energy levels and keep you full. Include a portion of fatty fish, add nuts to your salad, or use a vinaigrette made with olive oil.

- **Evening:** It's best to consume lighter fats in the evening to avoid indigestion and ensure a restful sleep. Consider a small portion of grilled salmon or a handful of walnuts.

2. **Portion Control:**

- **Portion Sizes:** Fats are calorie-dense, so controlling portion sizes is crucial. A general guideline is to keep fats to about 20-35% of your daily calorie intake. For a 2000-calorie diet, this translates to 44-78 grams of fat per day.

- **Measuring Portions:** Use kitchen scales to measure portions. For example, one tablespoon of olive oil contains about 14 grams of fat, and a small handful (about 1 ounce) of nuts contains roughly 14-17 grams of fat.

Calculating Daily Fat Intake

1. **Step-by-Step Calculation:**

- **Determine Your Daily Calorie Needs:** This varies based on age, sex, weight, height, and activity level. You can use an online calculator or consult a dietitian.

- **Calculate Fat Percentage:** Aim for 20-35% of your total daily calories from fats.

- **Convert Calories to Grams:** Since fat has 9 calories per gram, divide the calories from fat by 9 to get the number of grams. For example, if your target is 2000 calories a day and 30% from fat, that's 600 calories from fat. Dividing 600 by 9 gives you about 67 grams of fat per day.

Practical Tips for Including Fats in Your Diet

1. **Healthy Cooking Methods:**

- **Sauteing and Stir-Frying:** Use a small amount of olive oil or avocado oil.

- **Baking and Roasting:** Coat vegetables and lean meats with a light layer of oil.

- **Grilling:** Marinate with a healthy oil-based marinade to keep the meat juicy and flavorful.

2. **Smart Snacking:**

- Choose snacks that contain healthy fats, like a small handful of nuts, seeds, or a few slices of avocado.

- Avoid processed snacks high in trans fats and sugars.

3. **Mindful Eating:**
- Pay attention to hunger cues and eat slowly to allow your body to register fullness.
- Avoid emotional eating by addressing the underlying stress or boredom with non-food activities.

4. **Balancing Your Plate:**
- Ensure each meal contains a balance of macronutrients: carbohydrates, proteins, and fats. For example, a balanced meal might include grilled chicken (protein), quinoa (carbs), and a side salad with olive oil dressing (fats).

Avoiding Common Pitfalls

1. **Misleading Labels:**
- Be cautious of labels that claim "low-fat" or "fat-free," as these often contain added sugars and other unhealthy ingredients.
- Read the ingredient list to avoid trans fats, even in products claiming to be "0 grams trans fat" (if they contain less than 0.5 grams per serving, they can be labeled as such).

2. **Overconsumption:**
- Even healthy fats can contribute to weight gain if consumed in excess. Stick to recommended portion sizes.
- Balance fat intake with physical activity to ensure you're burning off excess calories.

Summary

Incorporating fats into your diet strategically can support weight loss and overall health. Focus on consuming healthy fats like MUFAs and PUFAs, moderate your intake of saturated fats, and avoid trans fats. Pay attention to the timing and portion sizes of your fat intake, and use mindful eating practices to maintain control. By understanding your daily calorie needs and how to calculate the appropriate amount of fat, you can enjoy the benefits of healthy fats without compromising your weight loss goals.

Remember, the key to a successful weight loss journey is balance and consistency. Including the right types of fats in your diet, at the right times and in the right amounts, can help you achieve and maintain your desired weight while supporting your overall health.

Is Indian Cow Ghee Superior to Other Fats?

Indian cow ghee, also known as clarified butter, has been a staple in Indian cuisine and Ayurvedic medicine for centuries. It is often touted for its health benefits, and many people believe that it is superior to other fats and can be consumed in large quantities without adverse effects. However, while ghee does have some unique properties and benefits, it's important to consider its consumption within the context of overall dietary balance and health.

What is Ghee?

Ghee is made by simmering butter to remove the water content, leaving behind pure butterfat. This process also removes most of the milk solids, making it a lactose-free option for those who are lactose intolerant. Ghee has a high smoke point, which makes it suitable for cooking at high temperatures.

Nutritional Profile of Ghee

- **Calories:** One tablespoon of ghee contains about 112 calories.
- **Fats:** It consists mostly of saturated fats (approximately 62%), with some monounsaturated fats (29%) and a small amount of polyunsaturated fats (4%).
- **Vitamins:** Ghee is rich in fat-soluble vitamins like A, D, E, and K.
- **Butyrate:** Ghee contains butyrate, a short-chain fatty acid that is beneficial for gut health.

Health Benefits of Ghee

1. **Rich in Antioxidants:** The presence of vitamins A and E in ghee acts as antioxidants that help in reducing oxidative stress.

2. **Anti-Inflammatory Properties:** Butyrate in ghee has anti-inflammatory properties and supports gut health.

3. **High Smoke Point:** Ghee's high smoke point (around 485°F or 252°C) makes it ideal for cooking at high temperatures without breaking down into harmful compounds.

Myths and Misconceptions

1. **Unlimited Consumption:** Despite its benefits, ghee is still a source of saturated fat and calories. Consuming it in excessive amounts can lead to increased cholesterol levels and weight gain.

2. **Superiority Over Other Fats:** While ghee has unique properties, it should not be considered superior to all other fats. A balanced diet includes a variety of fats, including monounsaturated and polyunsaturated fats, which are found in oils like olive oil and fatty fish.

Scientific Studies on Ghee

Several studies have examined the health effects of ghee, both positive and negative.

1. **Cardiovascular Health:**

- A study published in the "Journal of Food Science and Technology" (2015) indicated that ghee, when consumed in moderation, did not significantly alter serum lipid profiles in healthy individuals. However, excessive consumption could increase the risk of cardiovascular diseases due to high saturated fat content.

2. **Gut Health:**

- Research published in "Nutrition and Diabetes" (2012) highlighted the benefits of butyrate in ghee, which supports colon health and reduces inflammation in the gastrointestinal tract.

3. **Weight Management:**

- A study in the "American Journal of Clinical Nutrition" (2016) pointed out that while ghee can be part of a balanced diet, its high-calorie content means that portion control is crucial to prevent weight gain.

Practical Recommendations

1. **Moderation is Key:** While ghee has beneficial properties, it should be consumed in moderation as part of a balanced diet. The American Heart Association recommends that saturated fats make up no more than 5-6% of total daily calories.

2. **Cooking with Ghee:** Use ghee for cooking at high temperatures but be mindful of the portion sizes. A teaspoon or two can enhance the flavor and nutritional profile of your meals without adding excessive calories.

Conclusion

While Indian cow ghee does have some unique health benefits, it is not a miracle fat that can be consumed in unlimited quantities without health risks. Like all fats, ghee should be consumed in moderation as part of a balanced diet. The key to healthy fat consumption is variety and portion control, ensuring you get the benefits of different types of fats without overconsuming any one type.

In conclusion, ghee can be a valuable addition to your diet when used wisely. Its rich nutritional profile and cooking properties make it a versatile fat, but it should be enjoyed as part of a varied and balanced diet to support overall health and well-being.

CHAPTER TWENTY-ONE

VITAMINS AND TRACE ELEMENTS: AN OVERVIEW

Vitamins and trace elements are essential nutrients required in small quantities for various physiological functions. They play crucial roles in growth, development, and maintaining overall health. These nutrients must be obtained from the diet because the human body either cannot produce them or produces them in insufficient amounts.

General Information

1. **Definitions:**

- **Vitamins:** Organic compounds that are vital for metabolic processes. They are categorized into water-soluble (B-complex vitamins and vitamin C) and fat-soluble (vitamins A, D, E, and K) vitamins.

- **Trace Elements (Minerals):** Inorganic nutrients needed in minute amounts, such as iron, zinc, copper, selenium, iodine, fluoride, and manganese.

2. **Myths Associated:**

- **More is Better:** A common myth is that taking large doses of vitamins and minerals will enhance health, but in reality, excessive intake can be harmful.

- **Natural Sources are Always Better:** While natural sources are preferred, sometimes fortified foods or supplements are necessary to meet daily requirements.

3. **Jobs of Each Element:**

- Support metabolic functions, bone health, immune function, and energy production.

- Act as antioxidants to protect cells from damage.

- Facilitate enzyme activity and hormonal function.

4. **Natural Sources:**

- Found in a variety of foods including fruits, vegetables, meats, dairy products, grains, and nuts.

5. **Causes of Deficiency:**

- Poor diet, malabsorption, certain health conditions, and increased needs during periods of growth, pregnancy, or illness.

6. **Prevention of Deficiency:**

- Eating a balanced diet rich in diverse, nutrient-dense foods.

- Considering supplements when dietary intake is insufficient.

7. **Traditional Customs and Practices:**

- Many traditional diets were naturally balanced and included a variety of foods that provided necessary nutrients.

- Practices such as fermentation, sprouting, and preserving seasonal fruits and vegetables helped enhance nutrient availability.

8. **Excess of Nutrients:**

- Excess intake, especially from supplements, can lead to toxicity and adverse health effects.

Specific Vitamins and Minerals
Vitamin A
- **Definition:** A fat-soluble vitamin important for vision, immune function, and skin health.
- **Myths:** Eating lots of carrots will vastly improve eyesight.
- **Job:** Maintains healthy vision, skin, and mucous membranes.
- **Natural Sources:** Liver, carrots, sweet potatoes, spinach, and dairy products.
- **Deficiency Causes:** Poor dietary intake, malabsorption disorders.
- **Prevention:** Include a variety of colorful vegetables and animal products in the diet.
- **Traditional Practices:** Consuming liver and other organ meats, which are now less common.
- **Excess Effects:** Can lead to toxicity, causing liver damage, and central nervous system issues.

Vitamin B Complex
- **Definition:** A group of water-soluble vitamins that play a vital role in cell metabolism.
- **Myths:** B vitamins provide energy directly.
- **Job:** Aid in energy production, red blood cell formation, and nervous system function.
- **Natural Sources:** Whole grains, meats, eggs, dairy products, legumes, seeds, and leafy greens.
- **Deficiency Causes:** Poor diet, alcohol abuse, certain medications.
- **Prevention:** Consuming a varied diet with plenty of whole grains, meats, and vegetables.
- **Traditional Practices:** Traditional diets included whole grains and legumes, now often replaced by refined grains.

- **Excess Effects:** Generally excreted in urine, but extremely high doses can cause nerve damage (e.g., vitamin B6).

Vitamin C
- **Definition:** A water-soluble vitamin important for the growth, development, and repair of body tissues.
- **Myths:** Prevents the common cold.
- **Job:** Antioxidant, aids in collagen production, enhances iron absorption.
- **Natural Sources:** Citrus fruits, strawberries, bell peppers, broccoli, and spinach.
- **Deficiency Causes:** Poor intake of fruits and vegetables.
- **Prevention:** Regular consumption of fresh fruits and vegetables.
- **Traditional Practices:** Preservation methods like drying and pickling vegetables, which ensured year-round availability.
- **Excess Effects:** Can cause gastrointestinal disturbances like diarrhea.

Vitamin D
- **Definition:** A fat-soluble vitamin that is crucial for bone health.
- **Myths:** Sun exposure alone is sufficient for adequate vitamin D.
- **Job:** Regulates calcium and phosphate in the body, promoting bone and teeth health.
- **Natural Sources:** Fatty fish, fortified dairy products, and sunlight.
- **Deficiency Causes:** Lack of sun exposure, poor dietary intake.
- **Prevention:** Moderate sun exposure and consumption of fortified foods.

- **Traditional Practices:** Time spent outdoors and consumption of foods like cod liver oil.
- **Excess Effects:** Can lead to hypercalcemia, causing nausea, weakness, and kidney issues.

Vitamin E
- **Definition:** A fat-soluble vitamin that acts as an antioxidant.
- **Myths:** Prevents aging.
- **Job:** Protects cell membranes from oxidative damage.
- **Natural Sources:** Nuts, seeds, spinach, and vegetable oils.
- **Deficiency Causes:** Rare, but can occur in conditions that affect fat absorption.
- **Prevention:** Including nuts, seeds, and green leafy vegetables in the diet.
- **Traditional Practices:** Use of unrefined oils and whole foods.
- **Excess Effects:** Can interfere with blood clotting and cause bleeding problems.

Vitamin K
- **Definition:** A fat-soluble vitamin essential for blood clotting.
- **Myths:** Only important for blood clotting.
- **Job:** Helps in the synthesis of proteins required for blood clotting and bone metabolism.
- **Natural Sources:** Green leafy vegetables, fish, meat, and eggs.
- **Deficiency Causes:** Use of antibiotics, poor dietary intake.
- **Prevention:** Regular consumption of green leafy vegetables.

- **Traditional Practices:** Fermented foods like natto, which are rich in vitamin K2.
- **Excess Effects:** Rare, but can interfere with anticoagulant medications.

Iron
- **Definition:** A trace element necessary for the production of hemoglobin.
- **Myths:** Only needed by women and children.
- **Job:** Transports oxygen in the blood.
- **Natural Sources:** Red meat, poultry, fish, lentils, beans, and fortified cereals.
- **Deficiency Causes:** Poor diet, blood loss, malabsorption.
- **Prevention:** Including iron-rich foods and vitamin C-rich foods to enhance absorption.
- **Traditional Practices:** Cooking in cast iron pots, which added iron to food.
- **Excess Effects:** Can cause organ damage due to iron overload.

Zinc
- **Definition:** A trace element important for immune function and wound healing.
- **Myths:** Only beneficial for cold prevention.
- **Job:** Supports immune function, DNA synthesis, and cell division.
- **Natural Sources:** Meat, shellfish, legumes, seeds, and nuts.
- **Deficiency Causes:** Poor dietary intake, malabsorption disorders.
- **Prevention:** Regular intake of meat, seafood, and legumes.
- **Traditional Practices:** Consumption of organ meats and shellfish, now less common.

- **Excess Effects:** Can cause nausea, vomiting, and impair immune function.

Calcium
- **Definition:** A mineral crucial for bone health.
- **Myths:** Only needed during childhood.
- **Job:** Strengthens bones and teeth, supports muscle function and nerve transmission.
- **Natural Sources:** Dairy products, leafy greens, almonds, and fortified foods.
- **Deficiency Causes:** Inadequate dietary intake, vitamin D deficiency.
- **Prevention:** Regular consumption of dairy products and leafy greens.
- **Traditional Practices:** Consumption of bone broth, dairy, and small fish eaten whole.
- **Excess Effects:** Can lead to kidney stones and impaired absorption of other minerals.

Iodine
- **Definition:** A trace element essential for thyroid function.
- **Myths:** Only important for pregnant women.
- **Job:** Synthesizes thyroid hormones, which regulate metabolism.
- **Natural Sources:** Iodized salt, seaweed, fish, and dairy products.
- **Deficiency Causes:** Poor intake of iodine-rich foods, living in iodine-deficient areas.
- **Prevention:** Using iodized salt and consuming seafood.
- **Traditional Practices:** Coastal communities' diets rich in seafood.
- **Excess Effects:** Can cause thyroid dysfunction.

Selenium

- **Definition:** A trace element with antioxidant properties.
- **Myths:** More selenium means better immune function.
- **Job:** Protects cells from damage, supports thyroid health.
- **Natural Sources:** Brazil nuts, seafood, meat, and eggs.
- **Deficiency Causes:** Poor dietary intake, selenium-deficient soil.
- **Prevention:** Including selenium-rich foods in the diet.
- **Traditional Practices:** Consumption of a variety of nuts and seeds.
- **Excess Effects:** Can cause selenium toxicity, leading to hair loss, gastrointestinal issues, and neurological damage.

Summary

Vitamins and trace elements are crucial for maintaining optimal health. By understanding their roles, sources, and the importance of balanced intake, we can prevent deficiencies and support overall well-being. Traditional practices often provided a balanced nutrient intake, and modern diets can benefit from incorporating these age-old wisdoms to ensure we meet our nutritional needs.

Water: The Essential Nutrient

Water is a vital nutrient that plays a fundamental role in maintaining health and well-being. It constitutes a significant portion of our body and is involved in numerous physiological processes.

Functions of Water

1. **Hydration:** Water is essential for maintaining fluid balance in the body.

2. **Temperature Regulation:** It helps regulate body temperature through sweating and respiration.

3. **Nutrient Transport:** It facilitates the transport of nutrients and oxygen to cells.

4. **Joint Lubrication:** Water acts as a lubricant for joints and tissues.

5. **Waste Removal:** It aids in the elimination of waste products through urine and feces.

6. **Digestion:** Water is necessary for the digestion and absorption of food.

Dehydration and Excess

- **Dehydration:** Insufficient water intake can lead to dehydration, characterized by symptoms like dry mouth, fatigue, dizziness, and dark urine.

- **Excess Intake:** Excessive water consumption can result in water intoxication, causing electrolyte imbalances and potentially leading to hyponatremia.

Normal Water Consumption

- **Daily Requirement:** The general guideline is to drink about 8 glasses or 2 liters (approximately half a gallon) of water per day. However, individual needs may vary based on factors like age, activity level, climate, and health status.

Apps for Water Intake Reminder

- **Apps Available:** Various smartphone apps like WaterMinder, Hydro Coach, and Plant Nanny can help track and remind users to drink water regularly.

Role of Water Intake in Weight Loss

- **Hydration and Metabolism:** Adequate water intake supports proper metabolism and can help in weight management by enhancing calorie burning and reducing feelings of hunger.

- **False Sensation of Thirst:** Often, thirst is mistaken for hunger, leading to unnecessary calorie consumption. Drinking water before meals can help prevent overeating.

Guidelines for Healthy Water Intake

Water is essential for maintaining overall health, aiding in digestion, and supporting weight loss. Here are some practical guidelines for optimizing water intake throughout the day:

1. **Throughout the Day**: Drink water steadily throughout the day rather than in large amounts at once. This helps maintain hydration and supports metabolic processes continuously.

2. **Before Meals**: Consuming water before meals can help reduce calorie intake by promoting a feeling of fullness. This simple habit can aid in weight management.

3. **Sip by Sip**: Drink water sip by sip instead of consuming large quantities at once. This allows your body to absorb and utilize the water more effectively, reducing the risk of bloating.

4. **Glass, Not Bottle**: Take water by glass and not directly from a bottle overhead. This can help you monitor the amount you drink and encourages sipping rather than gulping.

5. **Small Sips After Meals**: Take only small sips of water immediately after meals to aid digestion without

diluting digestive enzymes. Increase your water intake 30 minutes after eating for optimal digestion.

6. **Morning Hydration**: Start your day with a glass of water to kickstart your metabolism and hydrate after a night's sleep. Adding a squeeze of lemon can provide a refreshing boost of vitamin C.

7. **Avoid Overhydration**: While it's important to stay hydrated, drinking excessive amounts of water in a short period can lead to a condition called water intoxication or hyponatremia, which can be dangerous. Listen to your body's signals and drink accordingly.

8. **Temperature Matters**: Room temperature or slightly warm water is often better for digestion compared to ice-cold water, which can slow down the digestive process.

9. **Herbal Infusions**: Occasionally, you can infuse your water with herbs like mint, basil, or fruit slices to enhance flavor and provide additional nutrients.

10. **Caution for Specific Conditions**: Patients with certain health conditions such as kidney disease, heart failure, or specific electrolyte imbalances should take water judiciously and follow their healthcare provider's advice regarding fluid intake.

By following these guidelines, you can ensure that you stay well-hydrated and support your overall health and weight loss goals effectively.

Conclusion

Water is indispensable for health, and maintaining adequate hydration is essential for overall well-being. By understanding the functions of water, recognizing the signs of dehydration and excess, and adopting appropriate intake methods, individuals can optimize their health and support weight management effectively. Individuals with specific health conditions need to consult healthcare providers for personalized hydration recommendations.

Importance of Fiber in the Body

Definition of Fiber

Fiber, also known as roughage or bulk, refers to the indigestible parts of plant foods. It passes relatively intact through the digestive system and plays a crucial role in maintaining health.

Importance of Fiber in the Body

1. **Digestive Health:** Fiber promotes regular bowel movements and prevents constipation by adding bulk to stool.

2. **Blood Sugar Regulation:** Soluble fiber helps slow the absorption of sugar and improves blood sugar levels.

3. **Heart Health:** Fiber can lower cholesterol levels, reducing the risk of heart disease.

4. **Weight Management:** High-fiber foods tend to be filling, promoting satiety and reducing overall calorie intake.

5. **Gut Health:** Fiber acts as a prebiotic, supporting the growth of beneficial bacteria in the gut.

How Fiber Helps in Losing Weight

- **Satiety:** High-fiber foods take longer to chew and digest, leading to a feeling of fullness and reducing the likelihood of overeating.

- **Calorie Density:** Many high-fiber foods are lower in calories per volume, making it easier to manage weight.

Removal of Fiber from Modern Diets

- **Processed Foods:** Many processed foods have had their natural fiber removed or reduced during manufacturing processes.

- **Fast Food Culture:** Convenience foods and fast foods often lack sufficient fiber content.

Rich Sources of Fiber

- **Whole Grains:** Brown rice, oats, quinoa.
- **Legumes:** Beans, lentils, chickpeas.
- **Fruits:** Berries, apples, pears (with skins).
- **Vegetables:** Broccoli, carrots, Brussels sprouts.
- **Nuts and Seeds:** Almonds, chia seeds, flaxseeds.

How to Incorporate Fiber-Rich Foods

- **Variety:** Include a variety of fiber-rich foods in your diet to benefit from different types of fiber.
- **Whole Foods:** Opt for whole grains over refined grains and whole fruits over fruit juices.
- **Quantity:** Aim for at least 25-30 grams of fiber per day for adults, gradually increasing intake to avoid digestive discomfort.

Additional Insights

- **Hydration:** Consuming adequate water alongside fiber-rich foods helps prevent constipation and supports digestion.
- **Slow Introduction:** Increase fiber intake gradually to allow your digestive system to adjust.

Conclusion

Fiber is a crucial nutrient for digestive health, weight management, and overall well-being. In today's modern diet, where processed and low-fiber foods are prevalent, consciously choosing fiber-rich options can significantly impact health positively. By incorporating a variety of fiber sources into daily meals and ensuring adequate hydration, individuals can support their digestive system, manage weight effectively, and promote long-term health.

As Amritha sat across from me, her brow furrowed with confusion and frustration, I could sense her overwhelming struggle to remember and implement all the dietary advice for her weight loss journey. Her eyes betrayed a mixture of hope and doubt as if wondering how she would ever manage amidst the sea of information. Taking her hands gently in mine, I assured her that she didn't need to burden herself with memorizing every detail. Instead, I shared a perspective that has resonated through generations: the wisdom of our ancestors.

"Amritha," I began softly, "our ancestors, hundreds of years ago, thrived on simple, natural foods. They lived healthy lives by embracing wholesome habits, far removed from the complexities of modern diets. Think of the fresh vegetables grown in home gardens, the nourishing grains milled nearby, and the pure ghee churned from indigenous cow breeds. These were not just food choices; they were a way of life—a harmonious blend of nutrition and tradition."

I paused, allowing my words to sink in, before continuing, "By embracing these ancient practices, avoiding modern and processed foods as much as possible, you're not just following a diet. You're reclaiming a natural rhythm that your body understands and appreciates. These practices, once unfamiliar, will gradually become your natural habits again. It's important to revisit these essentials of food intermittently, not as rules to follow rigidly, but as gentle reminders of our innate connection with wholesome living."

As I spoke, a glimmer of hope flickered in Amritha's eyes. It was as if she had found a beacon of simplicity amidst the chaos of information overload. She nodded slowly, a newfound determination replacing her earlier confusion. Together, we embarked on a journey to rediscover the nourishing traditions that had sustained generations before us—a journey guided not just by dietary guidelines, but by the wisdom of time-tested practices and a commitment to a healthier, more balanced life.

CHAPTER TWENTY-TWO

The Importance of Breakfast

"Breakfast is the fuel that powers your day, setting the tone for health, energy, and success. Never skip the most important meal of the day."

Importance of Breakfast

Breakfast is often hailed as the most important meal of the day, and for good reason. It kickstarts our metabolism, provides essential nutrients, and replenishes glucose levels after a night of fasting. A balanced breakfast sets the tone for the day by improving cognitive function, mood, and overall energy levels.

Myths Associated with Breakfast

1. **Skipping Breakfast Helps in Weight Loss:** Contrary to popular belief, skipping breakfast may lead to overeating later in the day and can disrupt metabolism.

2. **Not Hungry in the Morning Means You Shouldn't Eat:** It's crucial to fuel the body after waking up to maintain energy levels throughout the day.

Common Mistakes After Waking Up

- **Delaying Breakfast:** Waiting too long to eat after waking up can lead to excessive hunger and poor food choices.

- **Choosing Sugary Foods:** Opting for sugary cereals or pastries can cause a rapid spike and subsequent crash in blood sugar levels.

Scientific Explanation of a Good Breakfast

A good breakfast typically includes a mix of complex carbohydrates, protein, and healthy fats. Scientific studies have shown that consuming a balanced breakfast can:

- **Improve Cognitive Function:** Breakfast consumption has been linked to better memory, attention, and concentration.

- **Enhance Weight Management:** Regular breakfast eaters are more likely to maintain a healthy weight compared to those who skip breakfast.

- **Regulate Blood Sugar Levels:** A balanced breakfast helps stabilize blood glucose levels, reducing the risk of insulin resistance and diabetes.

Scientific Studies and Examples

- **Study:** Research published in the *American Journal of Clinical Nutrition* found that individuals who regularly ate breakfast had a lower risk of obesity and type 2 diabetes.

- **Ancestral Practices:** Ancient cultures often included fermented foods like idlis and dosas (made from fermented rice and lentils) in their breakfasts, which supported gut health and immune function.

Additional Insights

- **Timing:** Ideally, breakfast should be consumed within two hours of waking up to maximize its benefits.

- **Quality Over Quantity:** Focus on nutrient-dense foods rather than calorie-dense options to support overall health.

Conclusion:

Incorporating a nutritious breakfast into your daily routine can significantly impact your health and well-being. By understanding the scientific benefits and drawing inspiration from traditional food practices, you can cultivate habits that promote longevity, weight management, and overall vitality. Remember, breakfast isn't just about satisfying hunger—it's about fueling your body and mind for a productive day ahead.

In modern times, sticking to good breakfast practices can indeed be challenging, especially with busy schedules and hectic mornings. However, there are several practical strategies to ensure you prioritize breakfast and reap its benefits:

1. **Plan Ahead:** Prepare breakfast items the night before, such as overnight oats, chia pudding, or pre-cut fruits, to grab and go in the morning.

2. **Set a Routine:** Establish a morning routine that includes time for breakfast. Wake up a few minutes earlier if needed to avoid rushing.

3. **Keep it Simple:** Breakfast doesn't have to be elaborate. Opt for quick and easy options like yogurt with granola and fresh fruit, whole grain toast with nut butter, or a smoothie with greens and protein.

4. **Batch Cooking:** Cook larger batches of breakfast items over the weekend, such as muffins, breakfast burritos, or frittatas, and freeze them for quick reheating during the week.

5. **Portable Options:** Choose portable breakfasts like protein bars, hard-boiled eggs, trail mix, or whole fruit that you can eat on the go if necessary.

6. **Mindful Eating:** Make breakfast a mindful ritual. Sit down at a table without distractions to fully enjoy and

appreciate your meal.

7. **Hydration:** Start your day with a glass of water or herbal tea to hydrate your body and kickstart your metabolism before eating.

8. **Nutrient Balance:** Aim for a balance of macronutrients (carbohydrates, proteins, fats) in your breakfast to sustain energy levels and keep you full until your next meal.

9. **Avoiding Temptations:** Limit distractions such as checking emails or social media while eating to stay focused on your meal and avoid skipping it altogether.

10. **Seek Support:** Share your commitment to breakfast with friends or family members who can help remind you of its importance and encourage your healthy habits.

By incorporating these strategies into your daily routine, you can make breakfast a non-negotiable part of your morning, supporting your overall health, energy levels, and productivity throughout the day.

CHAPTER TWENTY-THREE

The Importance of Exercise on Weight Loss

The Role of Exercise in Weight Loss

Exercise plays a crucial role in weight loss by helping to burn calories, increase muscle mass, and boost metabolism. While diet is often the primary focus in weight management, incorporating regular physical activity amplifies the benefits and ensures sustainable results. However, there are numerous myths about exercise that often mislead patients.

Myths Regarding Exercise

1. **Myth: Exercise Alone Can Lead to Significant Weight Loss**

- **Reality:** Exercise is a critical component of weight loss, but it works best in conjunction with a balanced diet. Relying solely on exercise without dietary changes can lead to slower progress.

2. **Myth: You Need to Spend Hours at the Gym**

- **Reality:** Effective exercise doesn't require lengthy gym sessions. Even short, intense workouts or integrating movement into daily routines can yield significant results.

3. **Myth: Cardio is the Only Way to Lose Weight**

- **Reality:** While cardiovascular exercises are excellent for burning calories, strength training is equally important. Building muscle increases resting metabolic rate, helping you burn more calories throughout the day.

4. **Myth: Spot Reduction is Possible**

- **Reality:** You cannot target fat loss in specific areas of the body through exercise. Fat loss occurs uniformly across the body, influenced by genetics and overall body composition.

Integrating Exercise into Daily Work and Business

Modern lifestyles often leave little room for dedicated exercise sessions, but there are ways to incorporate physical activity into daily routines:

1. **Active Commuting:**

- Walk or cycle to work if possible. If you drive or use public transport, park farther away or get off a stop early to increase walking distance.

2. **Standing Desks:**

- Use a standing desk or take regular breaks to stand and stretch. This reduces sedentary time and encourages muscle activity.

3. **Take the Stairs:**

- Opt for stairs instead of elevators. Climbing stairs is an excellent cardiovascular exercise and strengthens leg muscles.

4. **Short Exercise Bursts:**

- Integrate short bursts of activity throughout the day, such as jumping jacks, squats, or desk exercises. Even five-minute intervals can add up.

5. **Walking Meetings:**

- Whenever possible, hold meetings while walking. This promotes physical activity and can enhance creativity and productivity.

6. **Household Chores:**

- Engage in vigorous household chores like cleaning, gardening, or washing the car. These activities burn calories and keep you active.

7. **Use Technology:**

- Utilize fitness apps or wearable devices to remind you to move and track your activity levels. Many apps offer short workout routines that can be done anywhere.

Importance of Small Movements

Small movements and activities throughout the day can significantly contribute to overall calorie expenditure and weight management:

- **Fidgeting:** Studies have shown that fidgeting and other small movements can increase daily calorie burn.

- **Posture:** Maintaining good posture engages core muscles and can prevent muscle fatigue and back pain.

- **Stretching:** Regular stretching improves flexibility and circulation, reducing the risk of injury and enhancing overall mobility.

Waking Up Early

Waking up early has several benefits for weight loss and overall health:

1. **Consistent Routine:**

- Establishing a consistent morning routine helps regulate your body's internal clock, promoting better sleep patterns and metabolism.

2. **Morning Exercise:**

- Exercising in the morning jumpstarts your metabolism and keeps it elevated throughout the day. It also ensures you don't skip workouts due to evening fatigue or unexpected events.

3. **Healthy Breakfast:**

- Waking up early provides time for a nutritious breakfast, setting the tone for healthier food choices throughout the day.

4. **Mental Clarity:**

- Early risers often experience improved focus and productivity, which can translate to better decision-making regarding diet and lifestyle.

Scientific Studies Supporting Exercise and Early Rising

1. **Indian Study:** A study conducted by the All India Institute of Medical Sciences (AIIMS) found that individuals who exercised regularly had a lower risk of obesity and related complications like diabetes and cardiovascular diseases.

2. **Overseas Study:** Research published in the *Journal of Applied Physiology* indicated that morning exercise improves metabolic health and increases overall physical activity levels throughout the day.

Conclusion:

Exercise is a vital component of weight loss, debunking common myths and highlighting practical ways to incorporate activity into daily life. Small movements and routine adjustments, such as waking up early, can have a profound impact on weight management and overall health. By understanding the importance of exercise and integrating it seamlessly into your lifestyle, you can achieve and maintain your weight loss goals effectively.

CHAPTER TWENTY-FOUR

UNDERSTANDING BASAL METABOLIC RATE (BMR) AND ITS ROLE IN WEIGHT LOSS

What is Basal Metabolic Rate (BMR)?

Basal Metabolic Rate (BMR) is the number of calories your body needs to maintain basic physiological functions at rest, such as breathing, circulating blood, and regulating body temperature. It represents the minimum amount of energy required to keep your body functioning while you are at rest and is a crucial component of your overall metabolism.

Myths Regarding BMR

1. **Myth: BMR is Fixed and Cannot be Changed**

- **Reality:** While genetics play a role in determining BMR, various lifestyle factors can influence it. Diet, exercise, and muscle mass can significantly affect your BMR.

2. **Myth: BMR is the Same for Everyone**

- **Reality:** BMR varies from person to person based on factors like age, sex, weight, height, and body composition. Men typically have a higher BMR than women, and younger individuals have a higher BMR than older adults.

3. **Myth: Eating Less Drastically Increases BMR**

- **Reality:** Severely restricting calories can actually lower your BMR, as the body adapts to conserve energy in response to perceived starvation.

Importance of BMR in Daily Life and Weight Loss

Understanding your BMR is essential for effective weight management. It helps you determine how many calories you need to consume to maintain, lose, or gain weight. By knowing your BMR, you can create a more accurate and personalized nutrition and exercise plan.

- **Caloric Needs:** Your BMR helps you estimate your total daily energy expenditure (TDEE), which includes calories burned through physical activity and digestion. This total helps in setting realistic calorie intake goals for weight loss or maintenance.

- **Weight Loss Strategy:** Knowing your BMR allows you to create a calorie deficit that is sustainable. A moderate calorie deficit can lead to gradual weight loss without triggering the body's starvation response.

- **Avoiding Overeating:** By understanding how many calories your body needs at rest, you can avoid consuming excess calories that can lead to weight gain.

How to Increase Your BMR

1. **Build Muscle Mass:**

- **Strength Training:** Incorporate weightlifting and resistance exercises into your routine. Muscle tissue burns more calories than fat tissue, even at rest.

- **Consistency:** Regular exercise helps maintain muscle mass and prevent metabolic slowdowns.

2. **Eat Enough Protein:**

- **Protein-Rich Diet:** Consuming adequate protein supports muscle repair and growth. Protein also has a higher thermic effect compared to fats and carbohydrates, meaning your body burns more calories digesting protein.

3. **Stay Hydrated:**

- **Water Intake:** Drinking enough water is essential for optimal metabolic function. Dehydration can slow down your metabolism.

4. **Eat Small, Frequent Meals:**

- **Meal Frequency:** Eating small, frequent meals can keep your metabolism active. Avoid long periods of fasting which can lead to a drop in BMR.

5. **Get Enough Sleep:**

- **Sleep Quality:** Poor sleep can negatively affect your metabolism. Aim for 7-9 hours of quality sleep per night.

6. **Manage Stress:**

- **Stress Reduction:** Chronic stress can lead to hormonal imbalances that affect metabolism. Practice stress-reducing techniques like meditation, yoga, and deep breathing exercises.

Common Mistakes That Lower BMR

1. **Skipping Meals:**

- **Inconsistent Eating:** Skipping meals or fasting for extended periods can cause your metabolism to slow down as your body tries to conserve energy.

2. **Extreme Calorie Restriction:**
- **Starvation Mode:** Severely cutting calories can lead to muscle loss and a decrease in BMR. A balanced approach to calorie reduction is more effective for long-term weight loss.

3. **Lack of Physical Activity:**
- **Sedentary Lifestyle:** Not engaging in regular exercise can result in muscle loss and a slower metabolism. Incorporate both aerobic and anaerobic exercises into your routine.

4. **Inadequate Protein Intake:**
- **Protein Deficiency:** Not consuming enough protein can lead to muscle loss and reduced metabolic rate. Ensure your diet includes sufficient protein.

5. **Poor Sleep Habits:**
- **Insufficient Rest:** Lack of sleep can disrupt hormonal balance and slow down metabolism. Prioritize sleep to maintain a healthy BMR.

6. **Dehydration:**
- **Insufficient Hydration:** Not drinking enough water can impair metabolic processes. Stay hydrated to keep your metabolism functioning efficiently.

Case Study: Understanding the Impact of BMR

To illustrate the importance of BMR, let's revisit Amritha's journey. After realizing that her previous weight loss efforts were not yielding the desired results, we conducted a comprehensive assessment, including calculating her BMR.

Amritha had been unknowingly under-eating and over-exercising, which had led her body to adapt by lowering her BMR. By adjusting her diet to include adequate protein and incorporating strength training, we focused on building muscle mass to increase her BMR. Additionally, we ensured she stayed hydrated and managed stress effectively.

Within a few months, Amritha began to notice positive changes. Her energy levels improved, and she started losing weight at a steady pace. Understanding and optimizing her BMR was a game-changer in her weight loss journey.

Conclusion

Basal Metabolic Rate (BMR) is a fundamental aspect of weight management and overall health. By understanding what BMR is and how it affects your body, you can create more effective and sustainable weight loss strategies. Avoid common mistakes that lower BMR and focus on methods to increase it, such as building muscle, eating adequate protein, staying hydrated, and maintaining a healthy lifestyle.

Understanding Your Numbers: Calculating BMR, BMI, and Calorie Needs

Understanding your body's basic needs is crucial for any weight loss journey. This chapter dives into three key metrics: Body Mass Index (BMI), Basal Metabolic Rate (BMR), and Daily Calorie Requirement. By calculating these numbers, you gain valuable insights into your body's energy expenditure and can set realistic goals for healthy weight management.

Body Mass Index (BMI): A Simple Screening Tool

BMI is a widely used tool to assess weight status for adults. It's calculated using a formula that considers your weight and height. While BMI doesn't differentiate between muscle mass and fat, it can provide a general indicator of potential weight-related health risks.

Calculating Your BMI:

There are two ways to calculate your BMI:

Online Calculators: Many websites offer free BMI calculators. Simply enter your weight in kilograms and height in meters, and the calculator will provide your BMI score.

Formula: Use the following formula and substitute your weight (kg) and height (m):

BMI = weight (kg) / height (m) squared

Interpreting Your BMI Score:

- Below 18.5: Underweight
- 18.5 - 24.9: Healthy weight
- 25 - 29.9: Overweight
- 30 or above: Obese

Limitations of BMI:

It doesn't distinguish between muscle mass and fat. Athletes with high muscle mass might fall into the "overweight" category despite having a healthy body composition.

It doesn't account for age, sex, or ethnicity.

Basal Metabolic Rate (BMR): Your Body's Engine

BMR is the minimum number of calories your body needs to perform basic functions like breathing, circulation, and cell repair, even at rest. It's the largest component of your total daily calorie expenditure.

Calculating Your BMR:

There are several equations to estimate your BMR, with the Mifflin-St Jeor equation being the most widely accepted:

For Men:

BMR = 10 * weight (kg) + 6.25 * height (cm) - 5 * age (years) + 5

For Women:

BMR = 10 * weight (kg) + 6.25 * height (cm) - 5 * age (years) - 161

Understanding Your BMR:
Your BMR is influenced by several factors:

- Age: BMR generally decreases with age as muscle mass declines.
- Sex: Men typically have a higher BMR than women due to more muscle mass.
- Body Composition: Muscle burns more calories than fat, so individuals with more muscle mass have a higher BMR.
- Daily Calorie Requirement: Tailoring Intake to Your Goals
- Your daily calorie requirement is the total number of calories your body burns each day. It takes your BMR into account and adds calories expended through activity.

Calculating Your Daily Calorie Requirement:
To estimate your daily calorie needs, multiply your BMR by an Activity Factor:

- Sedentary (little to no exercise): BMR x 1.2
- Lightly active (light exercise/sports 1-3 days/week): BMR x 1.375
- Moderately active (moderate exercise/sports 3-5 days/week): BMR x 1.55
- Very active (hard exercise/sports 6-7 days/week): BMR x 1.725
- Extremely active (very hard exercise/sports & physical job): BMR x 1.9

Using Calorie Needs for Weight Management:

- To lose weight, you need to create a calorie deficit. Aim to consume 500-1000 calories less than your daily calorie requirement.
- To maintain weight, consume roughly the number of calories your body burns each day.
- To gain weight, consume slightly more calories than your daily calorie requirement.

Remember:

These are estimates. Individual calorie needs can vary depending on factors like genetics and hormonal fluctuations. Consulting a registered dietitian or nutritionist can provide personalized guidance based on your specific goals and health conditions.

The Final Word: Numbers Are a Guide, Not a Dictator

While BMR, BMI, and calorie requirements offer valuable insights, they shouldn't be the sole focus. Focus on building healthy habits, incorporating a balanced diet, and engaging in physical activity you enjoy. These sustainable changes will lead to long-term health and weight management success.

CHAPTER TWENTY-FIVE

Optimal Eating Practices for Sustainable Health and Weight Management

In today's fast-paced world, maintaining a healthy diet can feel like a daunting task. However, by adopting simple yet effective eating practices, you can nourish your body, manage your weight, and promote overall well-being. This chapter explores the importance of balanced nutrition, meal timing, and mindful eating habits to support your health goals.

Balanced Nutrition: The 70% Rule

Eating well-balanced meals is key to providing your body with essential nutrients while managing caloric intake. The 70% rule suggests that your diet should consist of nutritious, whole foods that fuel your body without excess. This includes:

- **Protein-Packed Breakfast:** Start your day with a protein-rich breakfast to kickstart your metabolism and keep you full longer. Examples include eggs, yogurt, or protein smoothies.

- **Ideal Macronutrient Mix:** Aim for a balanced mix of protein, healthy fats, and carbohydrates in your meals. Proteins like lean meats, legumes, and fish provide essential amino acids for muscle repair and growth. Healthy fats from sources like avocados, nuts, and olive oil support heart health and satiety. Complex carbohydrates such as whole grains, vegetables, and fruits provide sustained energy and essential vitamins and minerals.

Avoid Suppressing Hunger with Unhealthy Substitutes

- **Mindful Choices:** Resist the urge to suppress hunger with unhealthy snacks like gutkha, pan, coffee, or tea. These can lead to empty calories, disrupt digestion, and spike blood sugar levels.

- **Fillers with Fiber and Protein:** Opt for fiber-rich fruits like apples, guavas, or snacks like chana (chickpeas) and sprouts. These provide satiety and essential nutrients without excess calories.

Gradual Reduction in Meal Size and Caloric Load

- **Portion Control:** Gradually decrease meal size to train your body to feel full with less food. This helps manage caloric intake and supports weight management goals.

- **Energy Balance:** Eat to fulfill your immediate energy needs without overloading your system. Avoid storing excess energy as fat by eating in moderation and respecting your body's hunger cues.

Historical Perspective: From Starvation to Abundance

In ancient times, many diseases stemmed from periods of starvation and nutrient deficiencies. In contrast, today's health issues often arise from overconsumption and imbalanced diets. By focusing on present nutritional needs and mindful eating practices, you can optimize health outcomes and save resources wisely.

Practical Tips for Everyday Success

- **Meal Preparation:** Plan meals ahead to include a variety of nutrient-dense foods.

- **Hydration:** Stay hydrated with water throughout the day to support metabolism and overall health.

- **Mindful Eating:** Avoid distractions while eating to savor and appreciate your food, which can prevent overeating.

Conclusion

Optimal eating practices are fundamental to achieving sustainable health and weight management. By prioritizing nutritious foods, balancing macronutrients, and respecting your body's hunger and satiety signals, you can foster a healthy relationship with food and support your long-term well-being.

CHAPTER TWENTY-SIX

IMPORTANCE OF TIMING MEALS FOR OPTIMAL HEALTH

The timing of meals plays a crucial role in maintaining overall health, supporting metabolism, and managing weight effectively. Here's a breakdown of why meal timing matters and the best practices to follow:

Importance of Meal Timing

1. **Regulates Metabolism:** Eating at regular intervals helps regulate your body's metabolism. Consistent meal times signal to your body when to expect fuel, optimizing energy expenditure throughout the day.

2. **Blood Sugar Management:** Spacing meals evenly can help stabilize blood sugar levels. This prevents spikes and crashes, which can lead to cravings and overeating.

3. **Supports Digestive Health:** Eating meals at appropriate times allows for proper digestion and nutrient absorption. This reduces the likelihood of digestive

discomfort and promotes gut health.

4. **Sustains Energy Levels:** Properly timed meals provide a steady source of energy, enhancing focus, productivity, and physical performance throughout the day.

Best Times to Eat

1. **Breakfast:** Ideally, breakfast should be eaten within an hour of waking up to kickstart your metabolism and replenish energy stores after fasting overnight.

2. **Lunch:** Aim to have lunch around midday, when your body's digestion and metabolic rate are at their peak. This meal should provide a balanced mix of nutrients to sustain energy for the afternoon.

3. **Dinner:** It's recommended to have dinner at least two to three hours before bedtime. This allows for adequate digestion before resting and promotes better sleep quality.

Snacking

1. **Mid-Morning Snack:** A light snack between breakfast and lunch can help maintain energy levels and prevent overeating during lunch.

2. **Afternoon Snack:** A small snack in the afternoon can curb hunger and stabilize blood sugar until dinner.

Timing for Weight Management

- **Caloric Distribution:** Distribute calories evenly throughout the day, with larger meals earlier when metabolism is higher and smaller meals or snacks later in the day.

- **Avoid Late-Night Eating:** Minimize eating close to bedtime to prevent disrupted sleep patterns and potential weight gain.

Tips for Effective Meal Timing

- **Consistency:** Establish regular meal times to maintain metabolic rhythm and support overall health.

- **Listen to Your Body:** Pay attention to hunger cues and eat when you feel moderately hungry, avoiding extreme hunger that can lead to overeating.

- **Hydration:** Drink water throughout the day to stay hydrated and support digestion.

Conclusion

Optimizing meal timing is essential for promoting metabolic efficiency, sustaining energy levels, and supporting overall health and weight management. By following a structured eating schedule and listening to your body's cues, you can cultivate healthy eating habits that contribute to long-term well-being.

The Significance of Meal Timing

This chapter underscores the significance of meal timing in maintaining metabolic health, supporting weight management, and enhancing overall well-being. Adopting appropriate meal timing practices can positively impact energy levels, digestion, and overall health outcomes.

In a bustling city not unlike ours, there lived a woman named Meera. Meera was a dedicated professional, managing a hectic schedule as a marketing executive. She prided herself on making healthy choices—or so she thought.

Every morning, Meera would start her day with a wholesome breakfast of oats and fruit, believing she was setting herself up for success. However, as the day progressed, her routine would unravel. Caught in back-to-back meetings and deadlines, Meera often skipped her mid-morning snack. By lunchtime, she was ravenous and found herself reaching for quick fixes—a greasy samosa from the office canteen or a sugary energy drink to keep her going.

Despite her best intentions, Meera's afternoons were a blur of caffeine and erratic eating. By evening, when she finally returned home exhausted, she would indulge in a late dinner—sometimes finishing as late as midnight. She would reassure herself that she hadn't eaten "anything bad" during the day, not realizing how her irregular eating patterns were impacting her waistline.

One evening, feeling unusually drained, Meera decided to visit me. As she poured out her frustrations, I listened attentively, nodding with understanding. I gently explained, "Meera, it's not always about what you eat, but when you eat it."

With empathy in my eyes, I illustrated how Meera's irregular meal timings and choices were disrupting her body's natural rhythm. "Our bodies thrive on consistency," I explained. "When we skip meals or eat at odd hours, it affects our metabolism and how our body processes food."

Meera realized with a pang of recognition that her sporadic eating habits were indeed contributing to her weight gain. I advised her on the importance of structured meal times and balanced nutrition throughout the day. I emphasized the significance of starting the day with a hearty breakfast, followed by regular meals and snacks to maintain energy levels and prevent overeating later in the day.

As Meera left my office that day, she felt a newfound sense of determination. She resolved to prioritize her health by adhering to a consistent eating schedule and making mindful food choices. Over time, with my guidance and her own commitment to change, Meera began to notice positive shifts—not just in her weight, but in her overall well-being.

Through Meera's story, I hope to convey a powerful lesson: that sustainable weight management isn't just about what you eat, but when and how you eat it. By honoring our body's natural rhythms and adopting healthy eating habits, we can pave the way towards a healthier, happier life.

CHAPTER TWENTY-SEVEN

CONQUERING THE NIGHT: FOOD, SLEEP, AND WEIGHT LOSS SUCCESS

Amritha sighed, rubbing her tired eyes. The glow of her laptop screen reflected in her glasses as the credits rolled on the latest episode. Another night lost in the captivating world of OTT, another bag of chips devoured alongside the plot twists. "Tomorrow," she thought for the hundredth time, "I'll start eating healthy and get a good night's sleep." But tomorrow never seemed to come. Does this sound familiar? Many people struggle with weight loss due to unintentional habits formed around nighttime activities like watching movies, late-night studying, and working. This chapter will explore the science behind how these habits impact weight loss and provide practical tips to conquer the night and achieve your weight loss goals.

Food Choices and Nighttime: The Calorie Conundrum

While the saying "calories in, calories out" holds true for weight loss, nighttime presents a unique challenge. Studies suggest that even when total calorie intake is the same, consuming a higher proportion of calories at night can lead to greater weight gain compared to a calorie-distributed diet. This might be due to the body's circadian rhythm, a 24-hour internal clock that regulates metabolism and hormone production. Research suggests our bodies are less efficient at burning calories and processing carbohydrates later in the day .

The Late-Night Snacking Trap

Amritha's nightly chip habit falls into the late-night snacking trap. These unplanned snacks often consist of high-calorie, processed foods that are low in nutrients and satiety. A 2019 study in the journal "Appetite" [3] found that people who snacked at night tended to consume more unhealthy fats and added sugars compared to those who didn't. This can lead to weight gain over time.

Sleep and Weight Loss: Partners in Progress

Sleep deprivation is another culprit in the weight loss struggle. When Amritha prioritizes late-night movies over sleep, she disrupts her body's natural production of hormones like leptin (which promotes satiety) and ghrelin (which increases hunger) . Lack of sleep can lead to increased cravings for high-carbohydrate and sugary foods, making it harder to resist unhealthy snacks. A 2017 study published in the journal "Sleep" [5] found that people who slept less than 7 hours per night were more likely to be overweight or obese compared to those who slept for 7 or more hours.

The Multitasking Myth: Focus on Food or Focus on Entertainment

Multitasking while eating, like Amritha does while watching movies, can lead to mindless overconsumption. Studies like one published in the journal "Appetite" suggest that people who are distracted while eating tend to eat more and feel less full compared to those who focus solely on their meals. This is because the body's satiety cues take time to register, and distractions can prevent us from recognizing these signals and stopping when we're full.

Conquering the Night: Practical Tips for Success

Here's how Amritha, and you, can break free from these nighttime habits and achieve weight loss success:

Establish a Cut-Off Time for Eating: Aim to finish your dinner at least 2-3 hours before bedtime. This allows your body ample time to digest food before sleep.

Plan Healthy Snacks: If hunger strikes after dinner, opt for nutrient-rich snacks like fruits, vegetables with hummus, or a small handful of nuts. Avoid processed foods and sugary drinks.

Create a Relaxing Bedtime Routine: Wind down before bed with activities that promote sleep, like reading, taking a warm bath, or meditation. Avoid screen time for at least an hour before sleep as the blue light emitted from electronic devices can disrupt sleep patterns.

Prioritize Sleep: Aim for 7-8 hours of quality sleep each night. A consistent sleep schedule helps regulate hormones and keeps your metabolism functioning optimally.

Mindful Eating: When you do eat, practice mindful eating. Focus on the taste, texture, and aroma of your food. Eat slowly and savor each bite. Put down your fork between bites and pay attention to your body's satiety cues.

Plan Meals and Snacks: Planning your meals and snacks in advance helps avoid unhealthy choices when hunger strikes. This can be especially helpful during movie nights.

Amritha's Journey to Healthier Nights

Gradually, Amritha noticed a difference. She found it easier to focus during the day and no longer felt sluggish in the mornings. The cravings for sugary snacks subsided, and she felt more satisfied after her meals. The weight loss, though slow and steady, was finally happening.

One Friday night, Amritha settled in for movie night with her friends. This time, however, popcorn with a sprinkle of herbs replaced the chips, and sparkling water took the place of sugary soda. While her friends munched on candy throughout the movie, Amritha enjoyed her healthy snacks, savoring each bite. Surprisingly, she didn't feel deprived. In fact, she found herself more engaged in the movie without the distraction of mindless snacking.

Building Sustainable Habits

Amritha's story reflects the power of small, sustainable changes. Remember, success doesn't come from drastic overnight changes. Focus on building healthy habits you can maintain long-term. Celebrate your non-scale victories – improved sleep, increased energy levels, and a better relationship with food. There will be slip-ups along the way – a late-night study session leading to pizza delivery, or a movie marathon with popcorn overflowing. Don't beat yourself up. Forgive yourself, get back on track with your healthy habits, and remember, progress over perfection is key.

The Power of Sleep for Weight Loss

Beyond regulating hormones like leptin and ghrelin, good sleep plays a crucial role in overall metabolic health. A 2013 study published in the journal "Diabetologia" found that even short-term sleep deprivation can impair insulin sensitivity, a key factor in blood sugar regulation. This can lead to increased cravings for sugary and high-carbohydrate foods, hindering weight loss efforts.

Furthermore, research suggests that sleep deprivation can negatively impact the body's ability to burn fat for fuel. A study published in the journal "Cell Metabolism" found that people who slept less than 5 hours per night burned 30% less fat compared to those who slept for 8 hours. This highlights the importance of prioritizing sleep for optimal weight management.

The Allure of Late-Night Movies and the Sleep Disruption Trap

Late-night movie marathons might seem like a harmless indulgence, but they can disrupt your sleep cycle in several ways. The blue light emitted from electronic devices like TVs and laptops suppresses the production of melatonin, a hormone essential for regulating sleep-wake cycles . This can make it harder to fall asleep and stay asleep throughout the night.

Furthermore, the stimulating nature of movies can leave your mind racing, making it difficult to wind down and prepare for sleep. A 2018 study published in the journal "Computers in Human Behavior" found that people who used electronic devices in bed reported poorer sleep quality compared to those who avoided screen time before sleep.

Making Sleep a Priority for Weight Loss Success

Prioritizing sleep is an investment in your weight loss journey. Here are some tips to ensure a good night's sleep:

Establish a consistent sleep schedule: Go to bed and wake up at the same time each day, even on weekends. This helps regulate your body's natural sleep-wake cycle.

Create a relaxing bedtime routine: Take a warm bath, read a book, or practice light stretches to unwind before sleep and make lights off around you for a comfortable sleep.

Optimize your sleep environment: Ensure your bedroom is cool, dark, and quiet. Invest in blackout curtains, earplugs, and a comfortable mattress.

Limit screen time before bed: Avoid using electronic devices for at least an hour before bedtime.

Get regular exercise: Physical activity can improve sleep quality, but avoid strenuous workouts close to bedtime.

By incorporating these tips and prioritizing sleep, you can create a foundation for successful weight loss and overall well-being. Remember, a good night's sleep isn't a luxury; it's a necessity for optimal health.

References:

[7] "Sleep Duration and Its Association with Risk Factors for Future Type 2 Diabetes in Adults: The Whitehall II Cohort Study" - Diabetologia (2013) Diabetologia journal

[8] "Sleep Deprivation and Impaired Insulin Action" - Cell Metabolism (2013) Cell Metabolism journal

[9] "Light, Melatonin, and Sleep Regulatory Systems: Lessons from Studies in Humans" - Cold Spring Harbor Symposia on Quantitative Biology (2010) Cold Spring Harbor Symposia on Quantitative Biology journal [invalid URL removed]

[10] "The Impact of Late-Night Smartphone Use on Sleep Quality and Cognitive Performance" - Computers in Human Behavior (2018) Computers in Human Behavior journal

CHAPTER TWENTY-EIGHT

SWEET INDULGENCES AND SELF-CARE: FINDING BALANCE WITH DR. LATH

The fluorescent lights of the clinic cast a dull glow over Amritha's usually vibrant face. Tears welled up in her eyes, threatening to spill over. "Is this it?" she croaked, her voice heavy with despair. "No more rosogollas? No more chocolate cake? Do I have to say goodbye to all my favorite things forever?"

I leaned back in my chair, a gentle smile softening the lines around my eyes. I understood Amritha's pain. Food wasn't just sustenance; it was a source of joy, a connection to memories, and a way to celebrate life's little victories.

Taking that away completely could feel like taking away a piece of herself.

"Amritha," I began, my voice warm and reassuring, "think of your body like a beautiful temple. It deserves to be treated with respect and care. But that doesn't mean you can't indulge in the things you love occasionally."

A flicker of hope ignited in Amritha's eyes. Could there be a way? Could she still have her cake and eat it too (well, a small slice anyway)?

I saw the shift and continued, laying out the four pillars of Amritha's sweet-tooth freedom:

The Power of Portion Control: "Imagine your favorite rosogolla," I said, "Not the entire box, but maybe just one or two. Savor each bite, appreciate the sweetness, and know that this small indulgence won't derail your progress."

Amritha pictured the glistening white spheres, a single bite satisfying her craving without guilt. It felt manageable.

The Art of Timing: "Think of these treats as special rewards," I explained. "Perhaps a small slice of cake after a particularly productive day, or a single rosogolla as an afternoon pick-me-up, when your energy needs a boost."

The idea of her favorite foods becoming rewards, not enemies, resonated with Amritha. It shifted her perspective from deprivation to mindful indulgence.

The Magic of Frequency: "Let's make these treats a rare occasion," I suggested, "Once a fortnight, or maybe even once a month. The anticipation will make them all the more special, and you'll appreciate them even more."

The thought of her favorite treats becoming a special event, a celebration of sorts, filled Amritha with a sense of control. It wasn't a complete banishment, just a conscious choice.

The Sweet Reward of Fitness: "Here's the secret weapon," I winked, "If you fit in a good workout session, you can enjoy a slightly larger treat afterwards. It becomes a reward for taking care of yourself."

Amritha's eyes sparkled. This was a win-win situation! Not only could she indulge, but it could also motivate her to exercise more.

I placed a hand on Amritha's, my touch conveying understanding and support. "Remember, Amritha," I said, "healthy living isn't about deprivation, it's about balance. It's about finding ways to incorporate the things you love into a lifestyle that nourishes your body and soul."

A tear escaped Amritha's eye, but this time, it was a tear of gratitude. I hadn't taken away her joy; I had shown her how to transform it into a tool for a healthier, happier life. As Amritha walked out of the clinic, the fluorescent lights seemed a little brighter, reflecting the newfound light in her eyes. She still had cravings, but now, she had the knowledge and tools to manage them, and that, in itself, was a sweet victory.

The Gut Whisperer's Guide to Weight Loss: How Your Microbiome Holds the Key

For decades, the focus of weight loss has been on calories in versus calories out. While this principle remains true, exciting new research suggests a hidden player in the weight management game: the gut microbiome. This intricate ecosystem of trillions of bacteria residing in your gut plays a far greater role than just digestion. Emerging evidence suggests a healthy gut microbiome can be a powerful ally in your weight loss journey.

The Science Behind the Buzz: How Gut Bacteria Impact Weight

Imagine a bustling metropolis within your digestive system. This metropolis, your gut microbiome, is teeming with a diverse population of bacteria, some beneficial and others not so much. These tiny residents play a crucial role in extracting nutrients from your food, regulating hormones that influence hunger and satiety, and even influencing your metabolism.

Here's how a healthy gut microbiome can potentially aid weight loss:

Nutrient Absorption: Different bacterial strains have varying capabilities for extracting energy from food. Beneficial bacteria are more adept at extracting short-chain fatty acids (SCFAs) from dietary fiber. SCFAs not only nourish the gut lining but also signal satiety to the brain, potentially reducing overall calorie intake [1].

Hormonal Harmony: Gut bacteria influence the production of hormones like leptin (promotes satiety) and ghrelin (increases hunger). A healthy microbiome may promote a hormonal profile that discourages overeating [2].

Metabolic Efficiency: Research suggests specific bacterial strains might influence how efficiently your body burns calories. A balanced microbiome may promote a metabolic environment conducive to weight management [3].

The Plot Thickens: The Pathophysiology of Gut Microbiome and Weight

The gut microbiome is a complex ecosystem constantly in flux, influenced by diet, lifestyle, and even environmental factors. Here's how an imbalanced gut microbiome might hinder weight loss:

Dysbiosis: This term describes an imbalance in the gut bacterial population, where "bad" bacteria outnumber the "good" ones. Dysbiosis can lead to increased inflammation, poor nutrient absorption, and altered hormone signaling, all of which can contribute to difficulty losing weight [4].

Leaky Gut: Chronic inflammation can damage the gut lining, leading to increased intestinal permeability, a condition known as leaky gut. This allows undigested food particles and toxins to enter the bloodstream, further promoting inflammation and potentially disrupting metabolism [5].

Common Mistakes that Sabotage Your Gut Microbiome

Many everyday habits can unwittingly disrupt your gut microbiome, hindering your weight loss efforts:

The Antibiotic Trap: While antibiotics are essential for fighting infections, they can also wipe out beneficial gut bacteria. Discuss alternative treatment options with your doctor when possible, and consider taking probiotics alongside antibiotics to minimize gut disruption [6].

The Sugar Rush: Excessive sugar intake feeds harmful bacteria, leading to an overgrowth and tipping the balance in the gut. Curb sugary drinks, processed foods, and refined carbohydrates for a healthier gut environment [7].

Stress, the Silent Saboteur: Chronic stress disrupts the delicate balance in your gut. Manage stress through techniques like yoga, meditation, or spending time in nature to create a gut-friendly environment [8].

The Fiber Famine: Fiber is the prebiotic fuel for beneficial gut bacteria. Unfortunately, modern diets are often low in fiber. Increase your intake of fruits, vegetables, and whole grains to nourish your gut microbiota [9].

Nourishing Your Inner Ecosystem: Strategies for a Healthy Gut Microbiome

Now that you understand the intricate link between gut health and weight management, here are some actionable steps to nurture your gut microbiome:

Embrace the Power of Probiotics: Probiotics are live bacteria that replenish the good guys in your gut. Consider incorporating probiotic-rich yogurt, kefir, or fermented vegetables into your diet. Discuss probiotic supplements with your doctor to find a strain suitable for your needs [10].

Befriend Fiber: Focus on including plenty of fiber-rich fruits, vegetables, and whole grains in your diet. Fiber acts as a prebiotic, feeding the good bacteria in your gut and promoting their growth [11].

Diversity is Key: A diverse gut microbiome is a healthy gut microbiome. Explore a wide variety of fruits, vegetables, and whole grains to provide a diverse range of nutrients for your gut bacteria to thrive on [12].

Prioritize Sleep: Adequate sleep is crucial for overall health, but it also benefits your gut microbiome. Aim for 7-8 hours of quality sleep each night to support a healthy gut environment [13].

Beyond the Chapter: A Final Word from Your Gut Whisperer (Continued)

There will be setbacks – a night of indulgence, a stressful week – but don't let these derail your progress. Be kind to yourself, and gently guide your gut microbiome back on track with healthy choices. Consistency is key. By incorporating these gut-friendly practices into your daily routine, you'll be nurturing a thriving ecosystem within you, one that can empower you on your weight loss journey and contribute to your overall well-being.

A Word from the Author

The world of gut health research is constantly evolving, offering exciting new insights into the connection between our gut bacteria and our health. While the evidence for the gut microbiome's role in weight management is promising, it's important to remember that it's just one piece of the puzzle. A holistic approach that combines a healthy diet, regular exercise, stress management, and adequate sleep is crucial for sustainable weight loss.

Think of your gut microbiome as a silent partner in your weight loss journey. By nurturing this vital ecosystem, you'll not only be supporting weight management but also promoting overall gut health, which can positively impact your digestion, immune function, and even your mood. So, listen to your gut whispers, embrace gut-friendly practices, and embark on a weight loss adventure fueled by the power of your inner ecosystem.

TAMING THE MINDFUL MONSTER: HOW BEHAVIORAL TECHNIQUES CAN CONQUER CRAVINGS

Amritha stared longingly at the leftover cake, a silent battle raging within her. "Just a small slice," her mind whispered. But Amritha knew this was the slippery slope to overeating. Weight loss isn't just about physical changes; it's also a mental battle. This chapter explores how behavioral techniques, specifically Cognitive Behavioral Therapy (CBT), can help you address the psychological factors that contribute to overeating and develop a healthier relationship with food.

The Psychology of Overeating: Beyond Calories

While calorie intake is important, emotional eating – using food to cope with stress, boredom, or sadness – can sabotage weight loss efforts. CBT recognizes this link between thoughts, emotions, and behavior. Through a series of practical techniques, CBT helps you identify unhealthy eating patterns triggered by emotions and develop healthier coping mechanisms.

The Power of Cognitive Restructuring

Imagine a negative thought like "I'm stressed, so I deserve dessert." This thought pattern can lead to emotional eating. CBT teaches you to challenge these negative thoughts and replace them with more empowering ones. For instance, "I can handle stress in healthy ways like taking a walk or talking to a friend." Over time, this cognitive restructuring can shift your mindset and help you make healthier choices.

Mindful Eating: Cultivating Awareness

Mindful eating is a core concept of CBT for managing weight. It involves paying close attention to the physical and emotional cues surrounding your eating experience. Here's how mindful eating can help:

Slow Down: Savor your food, chew thoroughly, and appreciate the taste and texture. This helps you feel satisfied with less food.

Identify Triggers: Notice situations that trigger unhealthy snacking. Are you bored? Stressed? Identify these triggers and develop alternative coping strategies.

Listen to Your Body: Learn to differentiate between physical hunger cues (growling stomach) and emotional cravings. Eat only when you're physically hungry, not emotionally driven.

Beyond the Therapy Room: Putting CBT into Practice

Here are some practical ways to incorporate CBT techniques into your daily life:

Keep a Food Journal: Track what you eat, how much you eat, and how you're feeling before, during, and after eating. This can help identify patterns and emotional triggers.

Challenge Negative Thoughts: When a negative thought arises, question its validity. Replace it with a more balanced and empowering thought.

Practice Relaxation Techniques: Deep breathing, meditation, and yoga can effectively manage stress and reduce cravings.

Reward Yourself: Celebrate non-scale victories like resisting a craving or trying a new healthy recipe.

Remember: CBT is a journey, not a quick fix. Be patient with yourself, and celebrate your progress. Consider seeking professional help from a therapist trained in CBT for personalized guidance.

The Final Bite: A Word from Your Weight Loss Coach

The human mind is a powerful tool, and CBT empowers you to use it effectively on your weight loss journey. By addressing the underlying emotional triggers, developing healthier coping mechanisms, and practicing mindful eating, you can break free from the cycle of emotional overeating and create a sustainable path to weight loss. Remember, you're not just changing your body; you're transforming your relationship with food and building a healthier, happier you.

CHAPTER THIRTY-ONE

AMRITHA'S JOURNEY TO HEALTH AND HAPPINESS

Amritha's story is a testament to the transformative power of dedication, resilience, and the right guidance in achieving health and happiness. When she first walked into my clinic, burdened by the weight of emotional distress and the looming threat of a crumbling marriage, little did she know that her journey towards weight loss would also become a journey of self-discovery and profound change.

Amritha's initial despair and confusion about where to begin were palpable. Her husband's dissatisfaction with her appearance due to obesity had shaken her deeply. But through our sessions, she not only learned about the science of nutrition and weight management but also uncovered the deeper emotional roots of her struggles with food and body image.

As Amritha embraced the principles outlined in this book—choosing nutrient-dense foods, balancing her meals, and incorporating regular physical activity—she began to see gradual but significant changes. Her weight loss journey was not without challenges. There were moments of doubt, setbacks, and the temptation to revert to old habits. Yet, each setback became a lesson in resilience and determination.

Two years into our journey together, Amritha achieved her desired weight. More importantly, she regained her confidence and saved her marriage. The emotional and physical transformation she experienced was not just about shedding pounds but about reclaiming her life and future.

Throughout this book, I have emphasized that weight loss is not a quick fix but a journey—a journey that requires patience, consistency, and self-awareness. Amritha's story illustrates this beautifully. She learned that sustainable weight loss is about making informed choices every day, nurturing healthy habits, and understanding that setbacks are a natural part of the process.

Amritha's success is a testament to the power of a holistic approach to health—one that combines nutrition, exercise, and emotional well-being. Her journey inspires us all to believe in our ability to change, to prioritize our health, and to embrace the journey towards a healthier, happier life.

As you embark on your own journey towards better health, remember Amritha's story. Let it be a beacon of hope and motivation. Believe in yourself, stay committed to your goals, and remember that with dedication and perseverance, anything is possible.

Here's to your health, happiness, and a future filled with vitality and well-being.

CHAPTER THIRTY-TWO

IGNITE THE SPARK: TAKING ACTION FOR A HEALTHIER YOU

You've reached the final chapter of this journey. You've explored the science of weight loss, delved into the power of gut health, and discovered the benefits of exercise and yoga. Now comes the most important step: taking action. This chapter is your personal cheerleader, a nudge to transform the knowledge you've gained into a life-changing experience.

The Starting Line is Here, But You Hold the Baton

This book has equipped you with the tools and knowledge to navigate your weight loss journey. However, the power to initiate change lies within you. Remember, a thousand-mile journey begins with a single step. Don't wait for the "perfect" moment to begin. Start today, even if it's with a small change like swapping sugary drinks for water or incorporating a short walk into your routine.

The Power of "Yet":

Negative self-talk is a common roadblock. We tell ourselves, "I can't," or "I'll start tomorrow." Instead, adopt the power of "yet." "I can't run a marathon yet, but I can walk a mile." This reframes your mindset, acknowledging the current state while holding onto the potential for growth.

Focus on Progress, Not Perfection:

Weight loss is a journey, not a destination. There will be bumps along the road – missed workouts, and unhealthy indulgences. Don't let these setbacks derail you. Focus on celebrating progress, no matter how small. Did you resist a craving? Excellent! Did you walk for 10 minutes longer than usual? Celebrate! These small wins pave the way for lasting change.

Find Your Tribe: The Power of Support

Weight loss can feel isolating. Surround yourself with a supportive network – friends, family, or online communities. Having people who understand your struggles and celebrate your victories can be a powerful motivator.

Embrace Self-Compassion:

Be kind to yourself. Weight loss isn't about punishment; it's about self-love and taking charge of your health. Forgive yourself for slip-ups and recommit to your goals.

Visualize Your Success:

Take a moment to visualize your ideal self – not just the physical changes, but the way you'll feel – energetic, confident, and empowered. Keep this image as your motivation when faced with challenges.

Celebrate Every Milestone:

Recognize and celebrate your achievements, big and small. Did you reach your first weight loss goal? Did you try a new healthy recipe? Take yourself out for a non-food reward to acknowledge your progress.

Remember, You are Not Alone

Millions of people are on this journey with you. You are strong, capable, and deserving of a healthy life. This book is a companion on your path. Refer back to it for guidance and motivation whenever you need it.

The Final Spark

Take a deep breath, close your eyes, and imagine the healthier, happier you. Now, open your eyes, and take that first step. With dedication, self-compassion, and the knowledge from this book, you can transform your life and achieve your weight loss goals. Remember, it's never too late to ignite the spark within you and create a healthier future. Start today, and watch yourself transform, one healthy choice at a time.

"Success is not about the destination, but the journey. Embrace the process, stay committed, and celebrate every small victory along the way."

In conclusion, remember that achieving a healthy weight and lifestyle is a marathon, not a sprint. Stay consistent, be patient with yourself, and rely on the support of your loved ones and mentors. Every step you take towards better health is a step towards a brighter future. Thank you for letting me be a part of your journey.

Dr. Shiv Kumar Lath

connect With Us And Continue Your Journey To Health

Dear Readers,

As you reach the end of this transformative journey through "Eat what you want, lose what you hate," I hope you've found inspiration, guidance, and practical advice to embark on your path to a healthier, happier life. Amritha's story, among others shared here, illustrates the power of determination and the impact of informed choices on achieving wellness goals.

To further support your health journey, I invite you to explore our range of other publications and resources tailored to address various health concerns:

E-Book Links and Online Consultation Links:

Understanding Diabetes

- Paperback:SEARCH "UNDERSTANDING DIABETES BY DR SK LATH " at the Notionpress website
-        [Buy   E-Book   at   Discounted Price](https://drsklath.mojo.page/the-diabetes-handbook)
- Hindi Edition : search "understanding diabetes in Hindi" by DR S K Lath at The Notionpress website

15 Secrets to Crack Any Exam

(My Own Biograpy And A source of motivation for all students and their parents) search at Notionpress website in India for both English and hindi

The Hypertension Handbook

-                    [E-Book](https://www.amazon.com/dp/B0CRDMD9Q5)

Connecting with Us

Contact Our Clinic in Jharsuguda:
Reach out to us directly at 9040881281 or 9438226633 for any inquiries or appointments.
Follow Us on Social Media:
Stay updated with the latest health tips, success stories, and updates:
-              [Facebook](https://www.facebook.com/diabetesjharsuguda?mibextid=ZbWKwL)
-              [Instagram](https://www.instagram.com/dr_lath_diabetes_expert?igsh=dDZ6bGVubXVyMTR1)
-

[YouTube](https://youtube.com/@patienteducation2101)
   - [Telegram](https://t.me/lathdr)
Online Consultations:
Book your online consultation through Lybrate for convenient and personalized healthcare support:
-        [Lybrate   Link   for   Online Appointments](https://www.lybrate.com/jharsuguda/doctor/dr-shiv-kumar-lath-general-physician)
Other Resources:

Check out our reviews and feedback on Just Dial to learn more about patient experiences and our commitment to quality care:

-        [Just   Dial   Review](http://jsdl.in/JR-RTHQHH11786051)

Join Our Weight Loss Program and Stay Connected!

Whether you're looking to manage weight, control diabetes, or improve overall well-being, our comprehensive approach integrates the latest medical insights with traditional wisdom. We believe in empowering individuals to take charge of their health through education, support, and personalized guidance.

Your feedback and engagement are invaluable to us. Share your thoughts, experiences, and success stories with us through social media, book reviews, or direct messages. Your journey inspires others to take their first steps towards a healthier lifestyle.

Remember, your health is your greatest asset. Invest in it wisely. Together, let's continue to strive for better health and a brighter future.

Warm regards,

Dr. Shiv Kumar Lath

Managing Diabetes Through A Healthy Diet

Living with diabetes can feel daunting, but with the right approach to diet and lifestyle, it's possible to achieve better blood sugar control and even reverse the condition in some cases. This chapter explores how adopting a balanced and mindful diet, as outlined in this book, can be transformative for diabetes management.

Understanding Diabetes and Diet

Diabetes is a metabolic disorder characterized by high blood sugar levels due to either insufficient insulin production (Type 1 diabetes) or ineffective use of insulin by the body (Type 2 diabetes). Diet plays a crucial role in managing diabetes because certain foods can affect blood sugar levels more than others.

Myth: Special Diabetic Diet Required

Contrary to popular belief, there is no specific "diabetic diet" that all individuals with diabetes must follow. Instead, the focus should be on a balanced diet that promotes overall health and helps stabilize blood sugar levels. By following the dietary principles outlined in this book—such as mindful eating, portion control, and choosing nutrient-dense foods—diabetes patients can effectively manage their condition.

The Role of Diet in Reversing Diabetes

Research has shown that sustained lifestyle changes, including dietary modifications, can lead to significant improvements in diabetes management and, in some cases, even reversal of the condition. Adopting a diet rich in whole grains, lean proteins, healthy fats, and plenty of fruits and vegetables can help stabilize blood sugar levels and reduce the need for medication.

Principles of a Diabetes-Friendly Diet

1. **Balanced Macronutrients:** Aim for a balanced intake of carbohydrates, proteins, and fats. Choose complex carbohydrates such as whole grains, legumes, and vegetables over refined sugars and processed foods.

2. **Fiber-Rich Foods:** Include plenty of fiber in your diet from sources like fruits, vegetables, whole grains, and legumes. Fiber helps regulate blood sugar levels and promotes digestive health.

3. **Healthy Fats:** Opt for unsaturated fats found in nuts, seeds, avocados, and oily fish. Limit saturated fats and avoid trans fats, which can increase the risk of heart disease.

4. **Portion Control:** Monitor portion sizes to prevent overeating and stabilize blood sugar levels. Use smaller plates and avoid seconds to manage calorie intake effectively.

5. **Regular Meals and Snacks:** Eating meals and snacks at consistent times throughout the day helps regulate blood sugar levels. Avoid skipping meals, as this can lead to fluctuations in blood glucose.

Reversing Diabetes Through Lifestyle Changes

By adhering to the principles of a healthy diet and incorporating regular physical activity, many individuals with Type 2 diabetes have successfully reversed their condition. This approach not only improves blood sugar control but also enhances overall health, including cardiovascular health and weight management.

Practical Tips for Diabetes Patients

- **Monitor Blood Sugar Levels:** Regularly monitor blood glucose levels as advised by your healthcare provider to understand how different foods and activities affect your body.

- **Stay Hydrated:** Drink plenty of water throughout the day to maintain hydration and support kidney function.

- **Consult with Healthcare Providers:** Work closely with your healthcare team, including doctors, dietitians, and diabetes educators, to tailor your diet and lifestyle plan to your specific needs and goals.

Conclusion

Managing diabetes through diet is not about strict restrictions but rather making informed choices that support overall health and well-being. By following the guidelines in this book and embracing a balanced and mindful approach to eating, individuals with diabetes can improve their quality of life, potentially reverse their condition, and enjoy long-term health benefits.

Annexure

Indian Weight Loss Meal Plan: Low-Calorie and Healthy Options

This sample meal plan provides low-calorie and healthy options for breakfast, lunch, and dinner, catering to an Indian palate. Remember, portion control is key, and adjust quantities based on your individual needs.

Breakfast (300-400 calories):

Option 1: Sprouts and vegetable cheela (made with lentils and vegetables) with a dollop of low-fat yogurt and chopped coriander chutney.

Option 2: Whole wheat dosa or uttapam with a lentil sambar and a side of chopped onions and tomatoes.

Option 3: Oatmeal (daliya) cooked with low-fat milk, nuts (almonds, walnuts), and a sprinkle of cinnamon and cardamom.

Option 4: Poha (flattened rice) stir-fry with vegetables like onions, peas, carrots, and a sprinkle of lemon juice.

Option 5: Two whole wheat bread slices with a mashed avocado and a sprinkle of chopped tomatoes and chili flakes.

Lunch (400-500 calories):

Option 1: Small bowl of brown rice with grilled chicken or fish, stir-fried vegetables, and a side of low-fat raita (yogurt with cucumber).

Option 2: Moong dal (lentil) soup with a side of whole wheat roti or brown rice salad with chopped vegetables, chickpeas (chana), and a light lemon vinaigrette.

Option 3: Vegetable biryani made with brown rice, a variety of vegetables (cauliflower, carrots, peas), and minimal oil or ghee.

Option 4: Salad with grilled paneer (cottage cheese), chopped vegetables, a light yogurt dressing, and a handful of sprouted moong dal.

Option 5: Two whole wheat chapatis with a simple vegetable curry (palak paneer, aloo gobi) and a side salad.

Dinner (400-500 calories):

Option 1: Baked salmon with roasted vegetables like broccoli, asparagus, and a side of brown rice or quinoa.

Option 2: Chicken stir-fry with mixed vegetables and a small portion of brown rice or whole wheat noodles.

Option 3: Vegetable kofta curry (vegetable dumplings) in a light tomato gravy with a side of whole wheat roti.

Option 4: Dal makhani (lentil dish) with a small portion of brown rice or a side salad with chopped cucumber, tomatoes, and onions.

Option 5: Tofu scramble with chopped onions, tomatoes, green chilies, and spices, served with a whole wheat roti or brown rice.

Snacks (100-150 calories):

1. Fresh fruits like apple, pear, guava, or banana.
2. A handful of nuts (almonds, walnuts).
3. Low-fat yogurt with sliced berries.
4. Vegetable sticks like carrots, cucumber, or celery with a low-fat yogurt dip.
5. Roasted makhana (foxnuts).
6. Small bowl of roasted chickpeas (chana).

Tips:

1. Use healthy cooking methods like grilling, baking, or steaming instead of frying.
2. Limit added sugar and salt in your meals.
3. Drink plenty of water throughout the day.
4. Consider incorporating healthy Indian spices like turmeric, cumin, and coriander for added flavor and potential health benefits.
5. Feel free to swap ingredients based on your preferences and dietary needs.
6. Consult a registered dietitian or nutritionist for a personalized meal plan tailored to your specific goals and health conditions.
7.

Here is a sample diet chart for various patient according to caloric needs

Sample 1500 Calorie Indian Diet Chart

This sample meal plan provides around 1500 calories and incorporates healthy Indian options. Remember, portion control is essential. Adjust quantities based on your individual needs and preferences.

Breakfast (300-350 calories):

Option 1: 1 cup (200ml) low-fat milk or unsweetened plant-based milk with ½ cup (75g) rolled oats (dalia), a handful of berries, and a sprinkle of nuts (almonds, walnuts) for added protein and healthy fats.

Option 2: 2 whole wheat roti or 1 cup (150g) brown rice flakes with 1 cup (250ml) low-fat curd (yogurt) and a sprinkle of chopped vegetables like cucumber, tomato, and onion.

Option 3: Vegetable (spinach, palak) omelet made with 2 egg whites and 1 whole egg, served with a side of chopped tomatoes and a whole wheat toast.

Mid-Morning Snack (100-150 calories):

1 medium apple or pear with a handful of roasted makhana (foxnuts) for a satisfying crunch.

A cup (240ml) buttermilk (chaas) with a pinch of cumin and chopped mint leaves for a refreshing drink.

½ cup (100g) sliced cucumber, carrots, or celery with a dollop of low-fat yogurt dip for a hydrating and crunchy snack.

Lunch (400-450 calories):

Option 1: Small bowl (1 cup/180g) brown rice with grilled chicken breast (100g) or baked fish (100g), stir-fried vegetables (broccoli, carrots, peas), and a side salad with a light lemon vinaigrette.

Option 2: Moong dal (lentil) soup (1 cup/250ml) with a side of 1 whole wheat roti (30g) or a vegetable salad with chickpeas (chana) and a light yogurt dressing.

Option 3: Vegetable pulao (mixed vegetable rice) made with brown rice (1 cup/180g) and a variety of vegetables, limited oil or ghee.

Afternoon Snack (100-150 calories):

A small bowl (1 cup/240ml) of low-fat yogurt with a sprinkle of chopped nuts and berries for a protein and fiber boost.

A cup (240ml) green tea with a squeeze of lemon for a refreshing and metabolism-boosting drink.

A handful of roasted chickpeas (chana) for a satisfying and protein-rich snack.

Dinner (400-450 calories):

Option 1: Baked salmon (100g) with roasted vegetables like cauliflower, asparagus (1 cup/150g), and a side of quinoa (½ cup/90g).

Option 2: Chicken stir-fry (100g chicken breast) with mixed vegetables (1 cup/150g) and a small portion (½ cup/90g) of whole wheat noodles.

Option 3: Dal makhani (lentil dish) (1 cup/250ml) with a small portion (1 whole wheat roti/30g) of brown rice (½ cup/90g) or a side salad with chopped vegetables.

Remember:

This is a sample plan. Feel free to swap ingredients based on your preferences and dietary needs.

Drink plenty of water throughout the day.

Cooking methods like grilling, baking, or steaming are preferable to frying.

Limit added sugar and salt in your meals.

Consult a registered dietitian or nutritionist for a personalized meal plan tailored to your specific goals and health conditions.

Sample 2000 Calorie Indian Diet Chart

This sample meal plan provides around 2000 calories and incorporates healthy Indian options. Remember, portion control is essential. Adjust quantities based on your individual needs and preferences.

Breakfast (400-450 calories):

Option 1: 2 whole wheat dosa or uttapam with a lentil sambar (1 cup/250ml) and a side of chopped onions and tomatoes.

Option 2: Oatmeal (daliya) cooked with 1 cup (240ml) low-fat milk, nuts (almonds, walnuts) for added protein and healthy fats (¼ cup/30g), and a sprinkle of cinnamon and cardamom.

Option 3: Scrambled eggs (2 whole eggs and 2 egg whites) with chopped vegetables like onions, tomatoes, and spinach (1 cup/150g), served with 2 whole wheat toast slices.

Mid-Morning Snack (150-200 calories):

1 medium banana with a tablespoon (15g) of peanut butter for a satisfying combination of protein and healthy fats.

A cup (240ml) of low-fat yogurt with a sprinkle of chopped fruit (berries, mango) and a drizzle of honey for a sweet and protein-rich snack.

A handful (30g) of mixed nuts and seeds for a satisfying crunch and a good source of healthy fats.

Lunch (500-550 calories):

Option 1: Small bowl (1.5 cups/270g) brown rice with grilled chicken breast (150g) or baked fish (150g), stir-fried vegetables (broccoli, carrots, peas), and a side salad with a light lemon vinaigrette.

Option 2: Moong dal (lentil) soup (1.5 cups/375ml) with a side of 2 whole wheat roti (60g) or a vegetable salad with chickpeas (chana) and a light yogurt dressing.

Option 3: Chicken biryani made with brown rice (1.5 cups/270g), a variety of vegetables (cauliflower, carrots, peas), and minimal oil or ghee.

Afternoon Snack (150-200 calories):

A bowl (1 cup/240ml) of cottage cheese (paneer) bhurji (scrambled) with chopped vegetables (onions, tomatoes) and a side of whole wheat toast (1 slice/30g) for a protein and fiber boost.

A cup (240ml) buttermilk (chaas) with a pinch of cumin and chopped mint leaves for a refreshing drink with gut health benefits.

A small bowl (1 cup/240ml) of sliced fruits like papaya or melon for a hydrating and vitamin-rich snack.

Dinner (500-550 calories):

Option 1: Baked salmon (150g) with roasted vegetables like cauliflower, asparagus (1.5 cups/225g), and a side of quinoa (1 cup/180g).

Option 2: Tofu stir-fry (150g tofu) with mixed vegetables (1.5 cups/225g) and a small portion (1 cup/ 180g) of brown rice noodles.

Option 3: Vegetable kofta curry (vegetable dumplings) in a light tomato gravy (1.5 cups/375ml) with a side of 2 whole wheat roti (60g).

Remember:

This is a sample plan. Feel free to swap ingredients based on your preferences and dietary needs.

Drink plenty of water throughout the day.

Cooking methods like grilling, baking, or steaming are preferable to frying.

Limit added sugar and salt in your meals.

Consult a registered dietitian or nutritionist for a personalized meal plan tailored to your specific goals and health conditions.

www.ingramcontent.com/pod-product-compliance
Lightning Source LLC
Chambersburg PA
CBHW051154130726
47988CB00005B/2119